MONSIGNOR
ROMERO

RECENT TITLES FROM THE HELEN KELLOGG INSTITUTE FOR INTERNATIONAL STUDIES

Scott Mainwaring, *general editor*

The University of Notre Dame Press gratefully thanks the Hellen Kellogg Institute for International Studies for its support in the publication of titles in this series.

Kevin Healy
Llamas, Weavings, and Organic Chocolate: Multicultural Grassroots Development in the Andes and Amazon of Bolivia (2000)

Ernest J. Bartell, C.S.C., and Alejandro O'Donnell
The Child in Latin America: Health, Development, and Rights (2000)

Vikram K. Chand
Mexico's Political Awakening (2001)

Ruth Berins Collier and David Collier
Shaping the Political Arena (2002)

Glen Biglaiser
Guardians of the Nation? (2002)

Sylvia Borzutzky
Vital Connections (2002)

Alberto Spektorowski
The Origins of Argentina's Revolution of the Right (2003)

Caroline C. Beer
Electoral Competition and Institutional Change in Mexico (2003)

Yemile Mizrahi
From Martyrdom to Power (2003)

Charles D. Kenney
Fujimori's Coup and the Breakdown of Democracy in Latin America (2003)

Alfred P. Montero and David J. Samuels
Decentralization and Democracy in Latin America (2004)

Katherine Hite and Paola Cesarini
Authoritarian Legacies and Democracy in Latin America and Southern Europe (2004)

For a complete list of titles from the Helen Kellogg Institute for International Studies, see http://www.undpress.nd.edu

MONSIGNOR
ROMERO

A Bishop for the Third Millennium

edited by

ROBERT S. PELTON, C.S.C.

with

ROBERT BALL AND KYLE MARKHAM

University of Notre Dame Press
Notre Dame, Indiana

Library of Congress Cataloging-in-Publication Data
Monsignor Romero : a bishop for the third millennium / edited by Robert S. Pelton,
with Robert Ball and Kyle Markham.
   p. cm.
   "From the Helen Kellogg Institute for International Studies."
   Includes bibliographical references and index.
   ISBN 0-268-03883-x (hardcover : alk. paper)
   1. Romero, Oscar A. (Oscar Arnulfo), 1917–1980.   I. Pelton, Robert S., 1921–
II. Ball, Robert L., 1946–   III. Markham, Kyle.   IV. Helen Kellogg Institute for
International Studies.
  BX4705.R669M667   2004
  282'.092—dc22

                                                    2004011376

Contents

Acknowledgments

I am grateful to Notre Dame's Helen Kellogg Institute for International Studies for its scholarly support.

Professor John Cavadini, the Chair of Notre Dame's Department of Theology, has generously underwritten the production costs for the color cover of this publication. Rebecca DeBoer of the University of Notre Dame has been most helpful in her editorial assistance.

It has been a pleasure working closely with Robert Ball and Kyle Markham in analyzing in depth the life and message of Archbishop Romero.

It is my hope and prayer that Archbishop Romero will serve as a model for Church leadership in the new millennium.

February 2004
Robert S. Pelton, C.S.C.
Notre Dame, Indiana

Introduction

ROBERT S. PELTON, C.S.C.

We all know that the rise of Christianity was leavened by the blood of its martyrs, but many of us believe—or perhaps we merely want to believe—that the "age of martyrs" is a relic of antiquity. Roman centurions no longer throw Christians to the lions, and persons professing to be Christians no longer burn their ostensibly less righteous brothers and sisters at the stake. Regrettably, we still hear of appalling incidents of hatred, violence, and persecution, but can't we conclude that these atrocities are isolated and atavistic aberrations? Isn't large-scale persecution of the faithful a remnant of the distant past?

Nothing could be farther from the truth. Far more Catholics died as martyrs during the 20th century than in any other century since the dawn of the Church. As Pope John Paul II wrote in his 1994 apostolic letter, *The Coming Third Millennium* (*Tertio Millennia Adveniente*): "The Church has once again become a Church of martyrs."

In May of the Jubilee Year 2000, John Paul II honored ten thousand "Witnesses of the Faith" who were martyred during the twentieth century. Even that number was only "a drop in the bucket," says Bishop Michael Hrynchyshyn, who headed the Vatican's Holy Year Commission for the New Martyrs. "The striking thing about this century is the huge number of martyrs on every continent," Bishop Hrynchyshyn told the Catholic News Service. "Hundreds of thousands of Christians died just because they were Christian."

The Witnesses of the Faith for whom the Holy Father prayed included many Protestant and Orthodox faithful as well as Catholics, in recognition of the fact that Christians of all denominations had suffered and died together. Addressing this reality in the "Christian Meaning of Human Suffering" (11 February 1984), the pope wrote:

> This glory must be acknowledged not only in the martyrs for the faith but in many others also who, at times, even without belief in Christ, suffer and give their lives for the truth and for a just cause. In the sufferings of all these people, the great dignity of man is strikingly confirmed.

In addition to their enormous number, the New Martyrs of our time differ from their predecessors in another highly significant manner: the overwhelming majority was not victimized by individuals, but rather by governments, armies, huge corporations, or other powerful and well-organized institutions. This was true in China's Boxer Rebellion, which killed forty thousand Christians at the beginning of the century; the Mexican Persecution (1917–1940); the Spanish Civil War; the Nazi death camps that killed Jews and others in almost incomprehensible numbers; the pervasive persecution of all faiths in the former Soviet Union; the "troubles" in Northern Ireland; the "ethnic cleansings"—largely along religious lines—in Kosovo and Iraq; the internecine cycle of attacks and reprisals between Jews and Muslims in the Middle East; and the state-sanctioned slaughter of hundreds of thousands of poor and marginalized South and Central Americans whose only offense was demanding their God-given human rights.

In *The Catholic Martyrs of the Twentieth Century*, Robert Royal observes: "Paradoxically, some of the most literate and advanced civilizations in the world witnessed the worst atrocities in the twentieth century." Gerald M. Costello, former editor in chief of *Catholic New York*, agrees: ". . . for all the knowledge they might have attained, some human beings—some nations and some movements as well—still lust for power. In so many cases the lust can be all consuming, overshadowing reason, erupting in hate, destroying lives in numbers that confound the mind."

Some of these Witnesses of the Faith are well known: Archbishop Oscar Romero; St. Maximilian Kolbe; Srs. Maura Clarke, Ita Ford, and Dorothy Kazel; Jean Donovan; and Fr. Gregory Grassi, among many others. Thousands of others were known only to their friends and families. This distinction is moot because all were martyrs in the true sense of the word: they gave their lives while bearing witness to the eternal truth of Christ and while doing his bidding in the world. In the words of *Lumen Gentium*: "Martyrdom makes the disciple like the Master."

Fr. Marco Gnavi, the secretary of the New Martyrs Commission for the Jubilee Year, offered the following reflection in an interview with the International Fides News Service:

Martyrdom in the 20th century spells out a message of love and the Gospel. It is also a choice for life, not for death. The new martyrs show how to live the Beatitudes in our day. These religious and lay people, men and women belonging to different churches and communions, tell us that it is worth opposing evil with daily choices of love, charity, reconciliation, and fidelity to the Gospel. Their example is a pressing call to have the courage of our Christian convictions, not to be afraid of exercising Christian virtues. And it is a call to unity in faith in Christ.

The Holy See is determined that these lessons in living the Beatitudes shall not be lost. In *Incarnationis Mysterium,* Pope John Paul II wrote: "The Church in every corner of the earth must remain anchored in the testimony of the martyrs and jealously guard their memory. . . . It is a testimony that must not be forgotten."

Ensuring that the powerful witness of the new martyrs is not forgotten is the raison d'être for the Archbishop Romero Lecture Series at the University of Notre Dame. Each year since 1987, we have come together in solemn remembrance of the great twentieth-century martyr and prophet Oscar Arnulfo Romero. This annual lecture series has been made possible through a grant provided by Eli Shaheen. It is cosponsored by Latin American/North American Church Concerns (LANACC) of the University of Notre Dame, the Helen Kellogg Institute for International Studies, and the Joan B. Kroc Institute for International Peace Studies.

Sadly, limitations of space make it impossible to include the entire treasure trove of reflections that have been presented throughout the years, but we hope that the representative selection that follows will share some measure of Archbishop Romero's enormous faith, commitment, and wisdom.

Perhaps it would be helpful to begin our quest with a brief and unavoidably incomplete portrait of the great martyr/prophet whom we honor and from whom we can learn so much about living the teachings of Christ in our daily lives—that man whom Bishop Pedro Casadaliga has called "Saint Romero of the Americas."

Archbishop Oscar Romero (1917–1980)

History records that Monsignor Oscar Romero y Goldámez, fourth archbishop of San Salvador, was assassinated while presiding at a memorial Mass in the Carmelite Chapel of the Hospital de la Divina Providencia on 24 March 1980. The archbishop was standing behind the altar, preparing the gifts of the offertory, when a neofascist mercenary fired a single shot through the chapel's open door. Archbishop Romero died within minutes from severe shock and blood loss. He died as a martyr and a prophet, as the greatest source of hope for millions of impoverished and oppressed Salvadorans, and as the greatest threat to the greed and arrogance of the oligarchy of fourteen families that ruled El Salvador as if it were their own private fiefdom.

History rarely mentions, however, the profound metanoia that transformed Romero from a timid advocate of noncontroversial virtues into a towering champion of the faith and of the faithful. We seldom hear how he discovered, in his own words, that "the word of God is like the light of the sun. It illuminates beautiful things, but also things which we would rather not see." Neither does history tell us how improbable Romero's Spirit-directed apostolate must have seemed to those who knew him best—or how improbable it must have seemed to Romero himself.

Oscar Romero was born on 15 August 1917 in Ciudad Barrios, a Salvadoran mountain town near the Honduran border. He was the second of seven children of Guadalupe de Jesús Goldámez and Santos Romero, who worked as a telegrapher. Although better off financially than most of their neighbors, the Romeros had neither electricity nor running water in their small home, and the children slept on the floor.

Since his parents could not afford to continue Oscar's education beyond the age of twelve, they apprenticed him to a local carpenter. Oscar immediately showed promise as a craftsman, but he was already determined to apprentice himself to the Carpenter of Nazareth. He entered the minor seminary in San Miguel at the age of thirteen; was promoted to the national seminary in San Salvador; and completed his studies at the Gregorian University in Rome, where he received a licentiate in theology. He was ordained in Rome in 1942. Unfortunately, his family could not attend his ordination because of World War II travel restrictions.

Although Fr. Romero hoped to pursue a doctorate in ascetical theology, he was called home to El Salvador in 1944 to help alleviate a severe shortage of priests. He initially served as pastor of a rural parish, but his exceptional leadership and organizational skills led him into administrative responsibilities. He was soon appointed rector of the interdiocesan seminary and secretary of the Diocese of San Miguel, a position he held for twenty-three years. Recognizing the evangelical power of radio long before most of his contemporaries, he convinced five local radio stations to broadcast his Sunday sermons in order to reach the huge number of *campesinos* who believed they were unwelcome in the churches of their "betters." Romero continued to rely on the electronic pulpit throughout the remainder of his life, making it a pillar of his ministries. He also served as pastor of the Cathedral Parish of Santo Domingo, as chaplain of the Church of San Francisco, as executive secretary of the Episcopal Council for Central America and Panama, and as editor of the archdiocesan newspaper, *Orientación*. These administrative duties seemed to be an ideal assignment for the shy and introspective Romero, who had serious doubts about his "people skills."

In 1970, he became auxiliary bishop for the Archdiocese of San Salvador, assisting the elderly Archbishop Luis Chávez y Gonzalez. Monsignor Chávez had been deeply influenced by the Second Vatican Council and was implementing a wide array of progressive reforms in pastoral work throughout his archdiocese. Many of these reforms—particularly lay leadership of catechists and Delegates of the Word—troubled Romero, who was then a doctrinal and social conservative and a staunch supporter of hierarchical authority. Indeed, a biographer described the Romero of 1970 as "strong-willed and seemingly born to lead, yet he submitted unquestioningly to a structure that encourages conformity." Romero diligently carried out the duties assigned to him by Archbishop Chávez, but he was not comfortable with several of the programs. It was with some relief that he left the archdiocese in 1974 to become bishop of Santiago de Maria, which includes his hometown, Ciudad Barrios.

Bishop Romero's hopes of escaping sociopolitical controversy were short-lived. Popular resistance to economic and political repression was growing as rapidly in Romero's diocese as in any other part of El Salvador. Although a few farm workers and laborers saw armed revolution as the only viable recourse, the vast majority was turning to the social teachings of the Church. Thousands joined Basic Ecclesial Communities (also known as Small Christian Communities) that sought to reform El Salvador in the light of the Gospels. The so-called "fourteen families" of the ruling aristocracy branded all such activities "communistic" and ordered the military to shoot strikers, union organizers, and human rights activists, especially teachers, students, nuns, and priests. The army's efforts were supplemented by mercenary death squads that roamed the countryside killing, raping, torturing, and looting with impunity, and then collecting cash bounties on every man, woman, and child they murdered.

Romero strenuously denounced violence against people who had "taken to the streets in orderly fashion to petition for justice and liberty," just as he had denounced "the mysticism of violence" being preached by the true revolutionaries. His words were not heeded. On 21 June 1975 Salvadoran National Guardsmen hacked five *campesinos* to death in the tiny village of Tres Calles. Romero rushed to the site to console the families and to offer Mass. Despite his lifelong determination to keep Church and politics completely separated, Romero felt compelled to publicly accuse the Salvadoran government of "grim violations of human rights." He also wrote a letter of protest to Colonel Arturo Armando Molina, head of the military dictatorship that ruled the nation, and he personally lodged a sharp protest with the local National Guard commander. The commander pointed his finger at Romero and replied, "Cassocks are not bulletproof." This was the first death threat directed at Romero, but it would be far from the last.

During his two years as bishop of Santiago de Maria, Romero crisscrossed his diocese on horseback, talking with *campesino* families to learn how he could best serve them. The reality of their lives horrified the bishop. Every day he discovered children dying from curable diseases because their parents could not pay for immunizations or basic medications; people who were paid less than half of the legal minimum wage, if they were paid at all; people who had been savagely beaten for "insolence" when they asked for long overdue pay; children who had been systematically denied educational opportunity so they would have no alternatives to becoming field laborers; and victims of literally hundreds of other forms of mistreatment.

Romero began using the resources of the diocese—and his own personal resources—to aid the poorest of the poor. Nevertheless, "the things we would rather not see" were teaching him that conventional charity was too little to help the recipients and too little to expect from the privileged. He wrote in his diary:

The world of the poor teaches us that liberation will arrive only when the poor are not simply on the receiving end of handouts from government or from churches but when they themselves are the masters and protagonists of their own struggle for liberation.

Similarly, in a pastoral letter released in November 1976, he reflected on the plight of the thousands of coffee plantation workers in his diocese:

The Church must cry out by command of God. God has meant the earth and all it contains for the use of the whole human race. Created wealth should reach all in just form, under the aegis of justice and accompanied by charity. . . . It saddens and concerns us to see the selfishness with which means and dispositions are found to nullify the just wage of the harvesters. How we would wish that the joy of this rain of rubies and all the harvests of the earth would not be darkened by the tragic sentence of the Bible: "Behold, the day wage of laborers that cut your fields defrauded by you is crying out, and the cries of the reapers have reached the ears of the Lord." [James 5:4]

Nevertheless, many still regarded Romero as a conservative both in his viewpoint and in his practices, especially in comparison to Archbishop Luis Chávez, who had reached mandatory retirement age. The government, the military, and the aristocracy were delighted to see the "safely orthodox" Romero replacing the activistic Chávez. Conversely, progressive pastoral leaders were hoping that the Vatican would choose Bishop Arturo Rivera Damas instead of Romero, whom they remembered as a harsh critic of their liberation theology initiatives. Clearly, both sides of the ideological spectrum had underestimated the scope of Romero's now-famous "conversion."

As Oscar Romero was being installed as archbishop of San Salvador, El Salvador was already at the brink of civil war. General Carlos Humberto Romero (no relation) proclaimed himself president of El Salvador following a blatantly fraudulent election. Eight days later, scores of people were killed when the police opened fire on thousands of demonstrators protesting election corruption. That same month, three foreign priests were beaten and expelled from the country, and a Salvadoran priest was abducted, beaten nearly to death, and thrown through the doors of the chancery.

On 12 March 1977 a death squad ambushed and killed Rutilio Grande, S.J., on a road from Aguilares to El Paisnal as "punishment" for his efforts to help peasants gain self-determination. The paramilitary group also machine-gunned the old man and young boy who were giving Fr. Grande a ride to the rural church where he planned to celebrate Mass. Hours later, the death squads assassinated another priest of the archdiocese, Fr. Alfonso Navarro. Romero rushed to El Paisnal and offered Mass in the house where the victims had been carried. Romero was deeply saddened by the murder of his friend and trusted aide, but he was also profoundly moved by the sugar-cane workers' testimony to Fr. Grande's works on their behalf and by their immutable faith that Jesus would send them a new champion.

At a funeral Mass in San Salvador Cathedral two days later, with one hundred priests officiating and thousands of mourners crowding the plaza, Monsignor Romero eulogized Fr. Grande and his two companions as "co-workers in Christian liberation." He went on to declare: "The government should not consider a priest who takes a stand for social justice as a politician or a subversive element when he is fulfilling his mission in the politics of the common good!" Both his choice of words and the force with which they were delivered made it clear that the Archbishop was delivering a message within a message.

Romero demanded that the president of El Salvador investigate the murders thoroughly, but the government's failure to deliver more than lip-service condolences reinforced the archbishop's growing belief that the right-wing government was an active collaborator in the atrocities. Realizing that his traditional reluctance to speak out on political issues had constituted de facto endorsement of repression and corruption, he notified the president that no representative of the archdiocese would appear with government leaders at public ceremonies. He also made the controversial decision to cancel Masses throughout the entire country the following Sunday except for a single national Mass on the steps of the cathedral. The faithful of all parishes were invited, and more than one hundred thousand attended. The event drew sharp criticism from the government, from the military, and from some bishops, but it united the pastoral leaders and the laity, and it signaled Romero's greater commitment to Catholic social tradition.

Although Fr. Grande's assassination had impacted Romero greatly, he knew all too well that it would not be the last of the atrocities. Four more priests were assassinated in 1979, along with many hundreds of catechists and Delegates of the Word. Military and police snipers fired into a peaceful protest march in downtown San Salvador, killing 21 and wounding 120 others. *Campesinos* were being murdered at the rate of three thousand per month, and their bodies were left to rot on roadsides as warnings to other "communists"—

a label that was, in some instances, used to justify the murder of children as young as four months. The courts consistently exonerated death squad members, praising them for "maintaining law and order" and for "protecting traditional values."

Beyond the overt violence, Monsignor Romero saw institutionalized social and economic injustice on a pervasive scale. Less than 2 percent of the population controlled 57 percent of the nation's usable land, while the sixteen richest families owned the same amount of land utilized by 230,000 of the poorer families. The use of the comparative rather than the superlative is intentional since the poorest families did not even have enough land to build a hut and were forced to sleep in ditches, alleys, or swamps. Mines and factories operated on the theory that it was cheaper to replace a dead or crippled laborer than to replace defective equipment or observe any safety standards. Approximately 60 percent of all babies died at birth, and 75 percent of surviving children suffered severe malnutrition.

Facing such realities, Archbishop Romero began to ask his now-famous questions—"How can Christians do such things to each other? What can the Church do to help the poor?" He found his answer in the realization that he had been called to Christ a second time, to the Christ who spoke to him in the Beatitudes. He found it also in the principles of Liberation Theology that he had once disputed; in the voices that had risen at the Second General Conference of the Latin American Episcopate at Medellín, Colombia; and in the simple yet powerful truth of Fr. Gustavo Gutiérrez's dictum "To know God is to do justice."

A cornerstone of his efforts to "do justice" was his establishment of a permanent archdiocesan commission that documented human rights abuses in an effort to find truth in a nation governed by lies. When he visited the Vatican in 1979, Archbishop Romero presented the pope with seven detailed reports of institutionalized murder, kidnapping, and torture. He also wrote to President Jimmy Carter, appealing to him as a fellow Christian to stop sending military aid to the Salvadoran government. "They will only use it to kill my people," Romero wrote. President Carter temporarily suspended aid in 1980, immediately after the murder of four U.S. churchwomen, but restored it soon afterward. President Ronald Reagan greatly increased shipments of money, weapons, and supplies to the Salvadoran military. In all, U.S. aid totaled $6.57 billion—an average of $1.5 million per day for twelve years. In human terms, it represents approximately $93,860 for each Salvadoran citizen killed by his or her own government.

Romero's pleas for international intervention were largely ignored. To his dismay, so were his calls for solidarity with his fellow bishops, all but one of whom turned their backs on him. He continued to plead for an end to oppression, for reform of the nation's deeply institutionalized structures of social and economic injustice, and for simple Christian decency. The rightists' only response was an increase in the death threats against Romero, repeated firebombings of the archdiocese's newspaper and radio station, and billboards and posters that read "Be a patriot—kill a priest!"

Romero had nothing left to offer his people except faith and hope. He continued to rebuild his radio station and to broadcast reports on conditions throughout the nation, to reiterate the Church's prophetic and pastoral roles in the face of horrendous persecution, to promise his listeners that good would eventually come from evil and that they would not suffer and die in vain.

There is little doubt that he was consciously speaking of his own suffering and death as well. He had long been aware that his vocation was a dangerous one. He saw himself denounced in the government-controlled media on an almost daily basis, and he received countless death threats. He responded by physically isolating himself from his colleagues and friends to the greatest extent possible, trying to prevent them from becoming secondary casualties, but he refused to be silenced. In his final Sunday homily, he said, "I have no ambition of power and because of that I freely tell those in power what is good and what is bad, and I do the same with any political group. It is my duty."

On 23 March 1980, after reporting the previous week's deaths and disappearances, Romero began to speak directly to rank-and-file soldiers and policemen: "Brothers, you are from the same people; you kill your fellow peasants. . . . No soldier is obliged to obey an order that is contrary to the will of God. . . . In the name of God, in the name of this suffering people, I ask you—I implore you—I command you in the name of God: stop the repression!"

These are among the most famous of Monsignor Romero's words, and they are the ones that best convey his Christianity, his ministry, and his personal character. In the 1988 Romero Lecture, Archbishop Luciano Mendes, president of the Brazilian Conference of Catholic Bishops, tells us that Archbishop Romero "was a man of nonviolence who paid a great price for his solidarity with the oppressed. His exhortation to the soldiers to lay down their arms and stop killing their own people was the last straw. Men of violence could not accept that a man of peace should ask people to stop killing."

The following evening, Archbishop Oscar Romero was assassinated in the chapel of Divine Providence Hospital. Only moments before his death, he had reminded the congregation of the parable of the wheat. His prophetic words:

> Those who surrender to the service of the poor through love of Christ will live like the grain of wheat that dies . . . the harvest comes because of the grain that dies. . . . We know that every effort to improve society, above all when society is so full of injustice and sin, is an effort that God blesses, that God wants, that God demands of us.

More than fifty thousand people gathered in the square outside San Salvador Cathedral to pay their last respects to Archbishop Oscar Romero on 30 March 1980. As they waved palm fronds and sang "You Are the God of the Poor," a series of small bombs were hurled into the crowd, apparently from the windows or balcony of the National Palace, which overlooks the cathedral's plaza. Cars strategically parked on all four corners of the plaza exploded into flames. The explosions were followed by volleys of gunfire that seemed to come from all four directions. Witnesses later reported seeing sharpshooters, dressed in civilian clothing, firing from the roof and balcony of the National Palace. More than seven thousand people took sanctuary inside the cathedral, which normally holds no more than three thousand. Many were crushed against fences and gates. Cardinal Ernesto Corripto Ahumado, who represented Pope John Paul II at the funeral, was delivering his tribute to Archbishop Romero when the first bomb exploded. The service was immediately postponed as hundreds of clerics tried in vain to calm the panicked mourners. As gunfire continued outside the cathedral, Romero's body was buried in a crypt below the sanctuary. The attack left forty mourners dead and hundreds seriously wounded.

In an eyewitness account published in the 31 March 1980 edition of the *Washington Post,* Christopher Dickey wrote: "A highly popular and controversial figure and an outspoken critic of the military that has long dominated this Central American nation, Romero was looked upon as one of the few people who could keep the violence-ridden society from plunging into all-out civil war."

Soon after Romero's death, El Salvador did indeed explode into full-blown civil war—a war which lasted for twelve bloody years, and which the United Nations Truth Commission has termed "genocidal." More than seventy-five thousand lives were lost, if one accepts the Salvadoran government's estimate, or nearly three times that many if we accept the conclusions of most international investigatory agencies. Ironically, by destroying much of El Salvador's industrial and transportation infrastructure, the war also destroyed much of the wealth that the aristocracy so zealously tried to horde. The Salvadoran Civil War did what wars do best: it victimized everyone.

It is not within our power to undo the unconscionable persecution of the Salvadoran people, of Monsignor Romero, or of the Latin American Church. But we can—and we must—remember this tragedy and we must learn from it. Let us never forget the lesson that Archbishop Romero offered us just days before he was martyred:

> I need to say that as a Christian I do not believe in death without resurrection. If they kill me, I will rise again in the people of El Salvador. . . . If they manage to carry out their threats, as of now, I offer my blood for the redemption and resurrection of El Salvador. If God accepts the sacrifice of my life, then may my blood be the seed of liberty and the sign that hope will soon become a reality. May my death, if it is accepted by God, be for the liberation of my people, as a witness of hope in what is to come. You can tell them that, if they succeed in killing me, I pardon and bless those who do it. A bishop may die, but the Church of God, which is in the people, will never die."

Many of our Romero Days speakers throughout the years have spoken eloquently about the enormous legacy that Archbishop Romero has left to the Church, to his homeland, and to our world—a legacy that is both so broad and so deep that it is almost impossible to fully define. Perhaps the greatest elements of this enduring legacy are the precious lessons that his example continues to teach to all who will listen. Specifically, he can teach us much about:

- Leadership ("Monsignor Romero: A Bishop for the Third Millennium")
- Solidarity and the promotion of awareness of institutional violence ("The Empowering Spirit of Archbishop Romero: A Personal Testimony")
- Protection of God-given human rights ("Monseñor Oscar Romero: Human Rights Apostle")
- Loyalty and commitment to the institutional Church ("Archbishop Romero and His Commitment to the Church")

- Awareness of contemporary martyrs ("Rutilio and Romero: Martyrs for Our Time")
- The role of Christian education, especially in the universities, to promote social justice ("Archbishop Romero's Challenge to U.S. Universities")

As Cardinal Rodríguez so sagely tells us, the witness of Archbishop Oscar Romero's life and martyrdom can teach us so much about living the teachings of Christ in our daily lives and can provide a veritable blueprint of a model bishop for the new millennium. Let us not squander this precious treasure.

1

Monsignor Romero

A Bishop for the Third Millennium

(2002)

OSCAR ANDRÉS CARDINAL RODRÍGUEZ MARADIAGA, S.D.B.

In a pastoral leadership course for bishops organized by CELAM that took place in Zipaquirá, Colombia, Father Anthony D'Souza asked, "What bishop from Latin America do you believe epitomizes the qualities of pastoral leadership?" Without hesitation, a Panamanian brother responded, "Monsignor Romero." This was in no way surprising to me. I was responsible for teaching these leadership courses throughout the continent, with fruitful results, and almost everyone I spoke with was in agreement.

CELAM's Publication Center has edited these pastoral leadership materials and published them in three volumes, the titles of which alone awaken the intellect: *Discover Your Power for Leadership*; *Success in Leadership;* and *Effective Leadership*.

One of the present problems in our society, especially in the political sphere, is the absence of authentic leaders. The bishop, as the pastor and guide of a community, is called to be a leader in the local church. But leadership cannot be improvised. The fact that many pastors from the [American] continent could feel like students and not teachers—could reflect together and listen to what a leader is—was a very enriching experience.

We could synthesize a great insight from three basic elements. A leader is: someone with a clear idea; someone who can communicate that idea; and someone who moves forward giving witness to it. From this perspective, the blessed John XXIII and Monsignor Romero are excellent examples. It is interesting to examine this topic from the perspective of the life and work of Monsignor Romero. We could also begin with the intriguing concept of "creative leadership," which Francois Houtart, the noted sociologist of the Catholic University at Louvain, has applied to Pope John XXIII's remarkable intuition to convoke an ecumenical council. According to Houtart, the existence of the social climate needed for a change in the Church to take place would have been useless were it not for someone who could incarnate this "creative leadership."

A creative leader should not only "institutionally embody the objectives" but also play the role of an educator. John XXIII epitomized these qualities remarkably. So many anecdotes show the "good Pope" to be a man who acted freely in the face of sometimes stifling institutional pressure, when this freedom was required by the evangelical virtues. His charisma as an educator has left us one jewel: the opening speech of the Second Vatican Council. At such a solemn occasion the pope managed to persuade the bishops of the world gathered there that the Church was at a transitional moment, and that the mission of the Council was to bring it up to date so that the bride of Christ could complete her mission in the modern world. And did he ever succeed!

What has happened, however, is that too many of the teachings and orientations of Vatican II have not yet been implemented. Despite the various apostolic duties of my pastoral ministry, I have never abandoned my initial vocation, which is teaching. I love to teach class. I hold the Moral Theology chair at the major interdiocesan seminary, Our Lady of Suyapa, in Tegucigalpa, Honduras. Each time I begin a new class with a new group of students, I ask them, "How many of you have read all of the documents of the Second Vatican Council?" Usually only one or two raise their hands. Then I say, "Don't consider yourselves modern. You are at least thirty-seven years behind the times!"

And the same thing happens, in a dramatic way, with lay groups. The Second Vatican Council is, in many ways, still brand new. It is for this reason that Pope John Paul II highlights the application of Vatican II as one point in the renewal of the life of the Church in *Tertio Millennio Adveniente*.

Much has been said about Monsignor Romero as a prophet and a martyr, and the testimony of his life has, without a doubt, inspired millions of men and women of all ages, even beyond the Church's borders. Here I wish to take up another, less publicized aspect of his life, but one which has come to the fore after the recent General Assembly of the Synod of Bishops, the theme of which was "The Bishop, Servant of Jesus Christ for the Hope of the World." I would like to share with you some contours of Monsignor Romero's rich personality, which will serve as a basis for presenting him as a model bishop for the third millennium.[1] The last part of the theme of the synod—the bishop as a servant of the Gospel of Jesus Christ "for the hope of the world"—moves me. After 11 September, that "black Tuesday" which has put before us in a brutal and verifiable way some fundamental questions, it is very difficult to talk about hope. It is also difficult to talk about hope in a globalized world in which even international finance organizations recognize that poverty is increasing and that the painful struggle of the marginalized and the excluded continues to grow in an unprecedented way.

The context in which Monsignor Romero was called by God to testify to hope was not much different. His people experienced the world this way, and a large portion of humanity continues to experience it this way today. What was his secret? I will try to approach this matter in two steps: remembering some elements of Monsignor Romero's personality, and exploring the deepest sense of his vision of Church. I will conclude with a reflection on the most radical form of giving witness to Jesus Christ: martyrdom.

Who Is This Timid Little Man Filled with God?

I clearly remember my first encounter with Monsignor Romero. I had been a bishop for barely three months when the Episcopal Conference of Honduras sent me as its representative to a conference on the Devotion to the Heart of Christ in Santo Domingo, Dominican Republic. It was in March 1979, exactly one year before his death. I was moved by his profound piety, his simplicity, and his humility. Today, after so many years have passed, I should admit that I had no idea then that I was in the presence of someone who would eventually become the most famous Salvadoran man in the history of that brother country, and—if you will allow me this daring statement—perhaps the most beloved martyr of the twentieth century, and a model who inspires numerous bishops who strive to take up the great challenges presented to us by the beginning of this millennium with faithfulness to God.

The pope, in his inaugural homily at the synod, pointed to some aspects of the bishop that are needed in today's Church which I would like to highlight. One of the aspects of this profile is the commitment to the poor. In the Final Message of the synod, the synodal fathers take up this challenge: "Just as there is a poverty that alienates, and against which we must struggle so that all who are subject to it can be liberated, so also can there be a poverty that liberates and harnesses energy for love and for service, and it is this evangelical poverty that we intend to practice. Poor before God the Father like Jesus in his prayer, his words, and his actions. Poor before all people, through a lifestyle that makes the person of Jesus attractive. The bishop is the father and the brother of the poor. He should not hesitate, when it is necessary, to become the spokesperson for the voiceless, so that their rights can be recognized and respected. In particular, the bishop should act in such a way that the poor feel at home in all Christian communities" (Final Message, 50). Was this not what Monsignor Romero did?

During his greeting in the San Salvador Cathedral on 6 March 1983, Pope John Paul II describes Monsignor Romero as ". . . the zealous pastor who was led by love of God and service to his brothers to the supreme sacrifice of his life in a violent way." The monsignor's priest friends, who knew him from the Diocese of San Miguel, remember him as a man of God, of fervent and disciplined prayer, possessing a great spirit of sacrifice, of love of the confessional and an overwhelming passion for the sharing of Jesus Christ and his Gospel through preaching and the written word.

They also recall some of his weaker attributes: a slightly difficult demeanor, impatience, some difficulty in dialoguing with some of the priests of the San Miguel Diocese, and shyness. All of his friends, without exception, remember him as a compassionate man, close to the poor and particularly generous, although still operating out of a model of assistance and incipient promotion of human flourishing at an individual level. In an editorial published in the weekly *Chaparrastique*, of which he was the director, Fr. Romero wrote: "This is the true Caritas, one that is not only content to feed someone out of a noble enthusiasm to give aid in an emergency situation, but one which, looking toward a better future, also teaches the poor how to work in order to earn their livelihood with dignity" (10 July 1965).

The qualitative leap with regard to social commitment would come when the Lord called him to the Episcopal See of San Salvador. It has become commonplace to call this change the conversion of Monsignor Romero. However, churchmen as close to him as were Monsignor Arturo Rivera Damas, his successor in the Salvadoran capital, and Monsignor Ricardo Urioste had a different opinion. They insist that his was not a conversion in the usual sense of the term, not a turning from the wrong path onto the correct path; it was, rather, the constant seeking of the will of God that led him to face bravely the structural sin that was crushing the little ones of his dear country.

Monsignor Gregorio Rosa Chavez recounts that in a radio interview he asked Romero, "Monsignor, they say that you have converted; what do you think of that?" Monsignor Romero's response was, "I would not say that it is a conversion so much as an evolution." It is the natural "evolution" of those who live in a permanent state of conversion, in total openness to God and neighbor.

In a book about Monsignor Romero written by Fr. Jesús Delgado, Monsignor Rivera writes in the prologue that he was not satisfied with the biographies written about his illustrious predecessor until *Oscar A. Romero, A Biography*:

Ten years ago Monsignor Romero was assassinated. During these years, many have written about the person, the work, and the words of the illustrious archbishop of San Salvador. None of these writings has completely satisfied me. Some authors have presented Monsignor Romero as a model Christian, who lives out his preferential option for the poor to the ultimate consequences, but they have erred in presenting this option as a political revolutionary weapon. Others attempt to defend the personality of the archbishop against his enemies' attacks at the price of denigrating their personalities. Almost all the writings that I have read to date situate the archbishop, who was the voice of the voiceless, in the political context of his time, which is not incorrect; however, they highlight this aspect so much that they lose sight of the essential dimension of his personality, the priestly dimension.

It is also interesting to note the opinion of the archbishop of Santiago de Maria, Monsignor Rodrigo Orlando Cabrera, who worked very closely with Monsignor Romero when Romero was the bishop of that small diocese in eastern El Salvador. In his book, *In Santiago de Maria I Happened upon Misery,* the pastor from Santiago writes: "When I returned from Medellín, I found him to be quite different. You could now speak to him about the social and political problems in the country. The authors of this book rightly affirm that the change in Monsignor Romero began in Santiago de Maria."

What happened next? Like John XXIII, Monsignor Romero allowed himself to be guided by the Holy Spirit.

To Feel with the Church

I began by talking about leadership, and to that end I indicated that a good leader has a clear idea and knows how to communicate it. Monsignor Romero chose as the theme of his episcopate *Sentir cum Ecclesia*. What image of Church did he have, and how did he communicate it to his flock? He did it, of course, through ordinary preaching. As we read in the Pastoral Plan of the Archdiocese for 1998–2003, "the words of Monsignor Romero resonated every Sunday from the cathedral of San Salvador." The next lines add: "But he also gave shape to his insights through four pastoral letters, and although they were addressed to the laity, they all speak of the Church. 'The Church of Easter' (April 1977) is the presentation of the new archbishop to his diocese. The three remaining letters were published on the occasion of Christ the King: 'The Church, the Body of Christ in History' (August 1977); 'The Church and Political and Popular Organizations' (August 1978), written together with Monsignor Arturo Rivera Damas; and the last one, which illuminates the path of the archdiocese with the light of Puebla, which is entitled 'The Mission of the Church in the Midst of the Country's Crisis' (August 1979)."

I will focus on the first pastoral letter because it was written by him from beginning to end. It was published only two months after the beginning of his pastorate in San Salvador. Through this, the archbishop's first official publication, we can clearly see the thinking of Cardinal Eduardo Pironio, with whom Monsignor Romero had a very close friendship. Actually, the letter contains many ideas from the retreat that the beloved Argentinean pastor offered the Central American Bishops at Antigua, Guatemala, while he was the secretary general of CELAM. It was the same retreat that Monsignor Pironio had offered at the Vatican for Pope Paul VI in 1974. The talks were published by the Library of Christian Authors (BAC) with the title *We Want to See Christ*. In the prologue, Pironio highlights what the Church described in the documents of Medellín is like. The expression "Easter Church" sums it up: a Church of cross and hope, of poverty and contemplation, of prophesy and service. This was the Church of Monsignor Romero's dreams—a church that exists to embody here and now the liberating force of Jesus' resurrection: "The church of Christ has to be an Easter Church. That is, a Church that is born of the Easter event and lives to be a sign and an instrument of that Easter in the midst of the world."

Focusing the Church on Easter is a brilliant move. The same thing happened with the writing of the Gospels, which are composed from the perspective of the Paschal Mystery; from this summit of the mystery of Jesus, the evangelists approach his teachings and his marvelous works. Romero writes that the Church is born of Easter, lives off Easter, and exists to proclaim and make present today the grace of Easter. To say Easter is to say unfailing hope, because it is based on Jesus' victory over sin and death, over Satan and his reign of evil. This is why the pope, in his homily at the Inaugural Mass of the General Assembly of the Synod of Bishops celebrated last year, said that Jesus Christ is our hope.

"The hope of the world is in Christ," affirms the pope. "In him the expectations of humanity find a real and solid foundation. The hope of every human being flourished from the cross, a sign of the victory of love over hate, of forgiveness over vengeance, of truth over lies, of solidarity over selfishness. We have the duty to communicate this salvific proclamation to the men and women of our time" (Inaugural Mass, n. 2).

Monsignor Romero: Servant of the Gospel of Jesus Christ Even unto Martyrdom

The officials and experts of the Congregation for the Causes of Saints have come upon a very complicated reality in studying the cause of Monsignor Romero. Because of this, the Congregation has asked the Archdiocese of San Salvador to describe in detail the social context in which Monsignor Romero exercised his pastoral ministry as archbishop of San Salvador. Those were years of brutal violence which drove him to utter that famous phrase, "It seems that my vocation is to go around picking up bodies."

We have become accustomed to the fact that in the investigations that are carried out in Latin American and Caribbean countries, the Catholic Church emerges as the most credible institution in the eyes of the populace. And it seems obvious to us that when there is conflict in a country and all the doors appear to be shut, the pastors of the Church are called upon to utter an authoritative word, to offer their good service, or even to assume a mediating role. We do not know of any public opinion polls that were conducted during Monsignor Romero's tenure, but there is one poll that is never wrong, and that is the attitude of the Salvadoran populace, awaiting Romero's evangelical words that illuminated the dramatic reality of that brother country every Sunday. Romero himself said that the word of God, of which he was a humble servant, is like the light of the sun, which illuminates beautiful things and things which we would rather not see. He would also warn against the temptation to divest the word of God of its power to transform history:

> The Bible alone is insufficient. It is necessary for the Church to take up the Bible and make it a Living Word again. Not in order to dole out psalms and parables word for word, but in order to apply it to the concrete situation in which the Word of God is preached at this time. (Homily, 16 July 1978)

The people understood this very well, and that is why they were glued to their radios every week. It is said that in towns and villages, during the eight o'clock Mass at the San Salvador Cathedral, you could walk the streets and verify that in almost every home Monsignor Romero's Mass was on the radio. We are in the presence of truly extraordinary events.

Perhaps one could think I am exaggerating by presenting Monsignor Romero as a model for a bishop in the third millennium. But Cardinal Carlo Maria Martini, archbishop of Milan, is in agreement, as he expressed in a pastoral letter written in 1983, a short time after the death of Monsignor Romero, entitled "Martyrdom, Eucharist and Dialogue."

With an enjoyable, incisive, and profound style, Cardinal Montini's successor in the Abrosian See recounts that a journalist once asked him which three cardinals most inspired him. In his response, Martini mentions Cardinal Augustine Bea, the great promoter of ecumenical dialogue and one of the "fathers" of the extraordinary conciliar document that is *Dei Verbum;* secondly he mentions Cardinal Josef Midnszenty, primate of Hungary, in whom he admires "his firmness in proclaiming things he considers just and the painful martyrdom he had to suffer for that." The third figure is not a cardinal, but rather Monsignor Romero. Martini explains why: "As bishop he never stopped speaking, making his voice heard among the people, the authorities, and the various political groups. His efforts to make himself heard by all was interrupted by death, which hit him at the most intense moment in the mission of a bishop: the celebration of the Eucharist." What follows is exquisitely beautiful: "He was not made a cardinal by title, but by the crimson of the blood he shed. He had said, 'martyrdom is a grace of God that I do not think I deserve. But if God accepts the sacrifice of my life, let my blood be a seed of liberation.'"

I cannot read this sentence by the archbishop of Milan without feeling motivated to share with you something in confidence. I do it as a Christian, as a cardinal who comes from a small, poor country that is forgotten, that only makes news when we suffer catastrophes; a nation that is very close to Romero's country not only geographically but also because of familial and cultural ties. A little more than a year ago, when I received my ring from the Holy Father's hands, I said, "I dedicate my tenure as cardinal to all the people of Central America and particularly the young, and those well-deserving pastors, like Monsignor Oscar Arnulfo Romero, Arturo Rivera Damas, Roberto Joaquin Ramos, and Marcos McGrath, who gave brave and generous witness to their love of the Church."

My second and last encounter [with Romero] was only one month before his death. A group of us, bishops from Central America, were in Panama working on a sketch of the Church's manual for social teaching that CELAM subsequently published with the title *Christian Faith and Social Commitment*. He had just returned from Belgium, where he had received an honorary doctorate from the University of Louvain. He stopped by to say hello to us, and he told us that he had selected *The Political Dimension of Faith from the Perspective of the Poor* as the theme of his doctoral dissertation. He told us: "I tried to explain how for us, in El Salvador, the key to understanding Christian faith is the poor. I said there that our Salvadoran world is not an abstraction. It is not one more instance of what is understood as 'the world' in a developed country like yours. It is a world which in its vast majority is made up of men and women who are poor and oppressed, and from this world of the poor we say that it is the key to understanding Christian faith, the action of the Church, and the political dimension of that faith and of that ecclesial action. The poor are the ones who ask us, what is the world and what is the service that the Church should offer?"

The following were his words on the day before his death, his last Lent before the definitive resurrection:

Already, in itself, Easter is the victory cry that says no one can extinguish that life, that Christ is risen and that death, all the signs of death, and hatred against Him and his Church can not win. He is victorious! But, just as he will flourish in an unending Easter, we must also accompany him throughout a Lenten season, and a Holy Week that is cross, sacrifice, martyrdom. And as he said: Blessed are those who are not scandalized by their cross. Lent, then, is a call to celebrate our redemption in that difficult complex of cross and victory. Our people are currently very capable of doing this. Their entire environment preaches the cross to us. But those who have Christian faith and hope know that behind this Calvary of El Salvador lies our Easter, our resurrection. And this is the hope of the Christian community. I have no ambition of power and because of that I freely tell those in power what is good and what is bad, and I do the same with any political group—it is my duty.

I wish to finish with a double citation of John Paul II, with whom I have been lucky enough to meet many times in a very friendly environment. In *Tertio Millennio Adveniente* he wrote, "At the end of the second millennium, the Church has once again become a church of martyrs" (no. 37). And in that same paragraph he adds, "It is a testimony that must not be forgotten."

What good this instruction of the Holy Father has done for us, and how it will inspire us at this tragic beginning of the third millennium! When economic and cultural globalization seems to be carrying everything away, the witness of the martyrs strengthens us on our journey. When so many means of social communication are mining our countries' cultures so rich in humane and Christian values, people like Monsignor Romero restore our pride in being Christians and in being Latin Americans.

There is another citation which is less well known, but just as important. We find it in the encyclical *Fides et Ratio*. I tell you sincerely, that when I read it, I saw in it a spiritual representation of the pastor whom we are commemorating today. It says:

I am thinking first of all of the witness of martyrs. The martyr, in effect, is the most authentic witness to the truth about existence. He knows that he has found in the encounter with Jesus Christ the truth about his life and no one or no thing can ever take away that certainty. Neither suffering nor a violent death will force him to separate from the adherence to truth that he has found in his encounter with Christ. This is why the witness of martyrs is accepted, listened to, and followed even in our day. It is the reason why we trust their word; we perceive in them the evidence of a love that has no need of long arguments to be convinced, since it speaks to each person of what they already perceive internally as true and long-sought-after. Certainly, the martyr produces great confidence in ourselves, because he articulates what we already feel, and he makes evident what we would also like to have the strength to express. (no. 43)

In pastors like Monsignor Romero, we have the figure of the "Bishop, who is a servant of the Gospel of Christ for the hope of the world." With bishops like him, the Church can truly be hope for the world!

NOTE

1. In his book *Povo de Deus* (*The People of God*) (Sao Paulo: Paulus, 2002), Father José Comblin also referred to Archbishop Helder Camara as a model bishop for the third millennium.

2

Martyrs, Heroes,
and the Contemporary Church

Latin America and the United States

(1988)

ARCHBISHOP LUCIANO MENDES DE ALMEIDA, S.J.

I was eyewitness to the facts of 30 March 1980 which happened at the funeral of Bishop Romero in San Salvador. Suddenly we heard and saw the explosion of a big bomb in the square in front of the cathedral. I have been witness to the suffering and anguish of the Salvadorian people, but also to their courage and maturity. El Salvador has suffered a long agony.

The assassination of Bishop Romero on 24 March 1980 shocked the world. He was a faithful witness to the Gospel, and he sealed that witness with his blood. Bishop Romero's life is a vivid reminder of the price that Christians are sometimes called upon to pay for their faith.

He said: "I know many are shocked by this preaching and they want to accuse us of forsaking the Gospel for politics, but I reject this accusation. I am trying to bring to life the messages of Vatican Council II and the conferences of Medellín and Puebla. Each week I go about the country listening to the cries of the people. Each week I ask the Lord to give me the right words to console, to denounce, to call for repentance."

This is the message that Romero preached through his life and words. We know it is the strong affirmation of the mission of the Church, defending and promoting the dignity of the human person in light of divine love. The joys and the hopes, the griefs and the anxieties of the men and women of this age, especially those who are poor or in any way afflicted—these, too, are the joys and hopes, the griefs and anxieties of the followers of Christ. Indeed, nothing genuinely human fails to raise an echo in their hearts. These are the words of the *Pastoral Constitution on the Church in the Modern World*. These are the griefs and anxieties of our age: that never has the human race enjoyed such an abundance of wealth, resources, and economic power, while such a huge proportion of the world's population is still tormented by hunger and poverty.

People have never been so aware of freedom; yet, at the same time, new forms of social and psychological slavery make their appearance. Romero wished, through the Church and in the light of Christ, to eliminate the misery of human beings and to cooperate in finding solutions to the problems of our time. What is the Christian reaction in the face of concrete oppression imposed on human dignity? The equal dignity of persons demands that just conditions of life be brought about. Excessive economic and social differences between the members of the human family are a scandal and militate against justice, equity, and the dignity of the human person. Every type of discrimination, whether social or cultural, whether based on sex, race, color, social condition, language, or religion, is to be overcome and eradicated as contrary to God's will.

We have to provide all men and women with everything necessary to lead a life that is truly human, such as food, clothing, and shelter; the right to choose a state of life freely and to raise a family; the right to education and to employment; the right to a good reputation; the right to respect; and the right to achieve these things in accord with the norms of one's own conscience. Protection of privacy and the right to freedom in matters such as religion are also a basic necessity. This is the message of Jesus Christ which Romero decided to preach. Jesus commanded his apostles to preach to all peoples the Gospel message so that the human race might become the family of God in which the fullness of the law would be love. Jesus not only announced universal fraternity—he made us brothers and sisters by participating in life itself, by sharing the spirit through sanctifying grace. His doctrine ultimately is not a question of violence or nonviolence, but of love or non-love. In his preaching he clearly taught the children of God to treat one another as sisters and brothers. He offered himself for all—"greater love has no man than this, that he lay down his life for his friends." Therefore, Romero proclaims the freedom of the children of God and liberation from the bondage of sin.

From the teachings of Jesus Christ, we know that Christians who neglect their temporal duties are neglecting their duties towards neighbor and even toward God, thus jeopardizing their eternal salvation. All pastors should remember, also, that by their daily conduct and concern they are revealing the face of the Church to the world in their lives and words. The Church is an unspent fountain of those virtues which the modern world most needs.

Romero always spoke the truth about the situation of oppression and repression being lived by the poorest of the poor—even risking his life to do so. He sought to bring out this conflictual reality from a perspective of faith, of response to the cries and hopes of his people and especially from the perspective of a prayer relationship to the Lord. Romero knew that social injustice is not merely one of the causes of violence—it is above all the first radical form of violence. In efforts to deter the escalation of violence, the Christian conscience excludes resorting to violent ways and includes appeal to fraternity. The permanent firmness of attitude toward the unjust structures involves intelligence, determination, affection, and a capacity to react in a strong but peaceful manner.

Bishop Oscar Romero was a strong defender of justice. Like Jesus, he denounced and called to task those who repress and assassinate the poor who struggle for their life and rights. Therefore, he launched a process of solidarity. He knew how to respond to the reality of the Church in his own faith and in solidarity with others. Romero understood quite well that the root of this process is the solidarity of the Church with the poor and the oppressed, and he stated that in a totally radical way. He said, ". . . the Church suffers the lot of the poor, which is persecution. Our Church is proud that the blood of its priests, catechists, and communities has been mixed in with the blood of the massacred people. My position as pastor obliges me to stand in solidarity with everyone who suffers and to back every effort to promote the dignity of human beings."

Bishop Romero was the friend, the father, the brother, and the defender of the poor and oppressed, of the peasants, the underemployed workers, and the slum dwellers. His fervent faith in God and his total giving of himself to Christ led him to see these people as Christ himself and to defend the cause of the poor as God's cause. Therefore, the question that permeates Bishop Romero's pastoral concern is the question the Lord put to Cain: "What have you done to your brother?" [Gen. 4]. It was his concern with this question that eventually cost Bishop Romero his life.

In Latin America, this is a serious issue because of the institutionalized violence which most of the continent suffers. This violence is both the cause for and the product of a situation where the vast majority of men, women, and children are deprived of the basic necessities of life. This deprivation is not due to natural catastrophes or laziness or the will of God, but is an integral part of the social, economic, and political systems which accept as normal a situation in which the vast majority of people constitute an impoverished subforce at the service of the privileged minority. Such violence frequently finds its legitimization in the status quo politics, attitudes, and values which are communicated through the media and through many forms of religious expression. The Church is too often called upon and expected to give its blessing to this state of affairs. When such legitimization is not forthcoming, or not sufficiently widespread, repressive violence is employed by the security forces to crush the aspirations of the majority of the men and women who seek a fuller participation in the social, economic, and cultural life of the country.

All these should be borne in mind when trying to understand the life and death of Bishop Romero. However, there is one more element which is essential to grasp: the international connection. Stable, anticommunist governments are seen as vital in the event of a communist threat to western democracy. In this sense, any social conflict in Latin America is considered to be potentially dangerous. We confuse popular aspiration for human dignity and the right to participate in one's own destiny with subversive communism. The truth is that many of the struggles for liberation in Latin America have little or nothing to do with communism. If they eventually become so, it is only after the hope for change has been lost. Liberation struggles are movements of men and women in search of their God-given dignity, a dignity which historically has been denied them by the violence of the political system. This is the context in which we need to place Bishop Romero's life.

Some people might ask why a churchman need concern himself with such mundane matters. It is precisely the Church's religious character and mission which generate a role (expressed in the *Gaudium et Spes* as "light and energy") that can serve to consolidate the human community according to divine law. It is the task of the Church to gather to itself all that is human in the struggle of the people, and above all the struggle of the poor, especially when they seek their legitimate rights. For this reason Bishop Romero, in keeping with the words of Medellín, found himself encouraging all those forces among the people aimed at creating and developing their own basic organizations to recover and consolidate their rights, and to search for true justice. In other words, Romero believed, along with Pope Paul, that the economic, social, political, and cultural hopes of humanity are not alien to the definitive liberation achieved in Jesus Christ. Liberation theology was born from reflections on the structurally institutionalized violence and injustice that characterizes most of Latin America.

In El Salvador, Bishop Romero's position brought him into inevitable conflict with both institutionalized and repressive violence. Why this violence? Some statistics may help to explain it. Of a total population of five million, 2 percent control 57 percent of the usable land, while 91 percent of the people occupy only 21 percent of the land; sixteen families own the same amount of land as is utilized by 230,000 rural families; 75 percent of the children suffer from serious malnutrition; 60 percent of the children die at birth. Only 57 percent of the population has safe drinking water and half of the people cannot read or write. Given such a social reality, it is not necessary to invent the phantasm of communism to justify the desire for change. But that is what much of current foreign policy has done. This fact, reinforced by national self-interest in El Salvador, has made any real change impossible. In fact, it has caused a violent revolution that has claimed about eighty thousand lives since 1979. One of the victims of this violence was Bishop Romero himself—shot dead by hired gunmen while saying Mass. Even now, no one has been brought to trial for this crime, although it is widely known that the intellectual authors of the crime were people in high positions in El Salvador's government.

Still, Bishop Romero's work continues in the struggle for justice and liberation which he inspired by his life and sacrifice. He was a man of nonviolence who paid a great price for his solidarity with the oppressed. His exhortation to the soldiers to lay down their arms and stop killing their own people was the last straw. Men of violence could not accept that a man of peace should ask people to stop killing.

Where does Bishop Romero live today? He lives in the communities of refugees, among the poor, in the liturgical celebrations, in the meetings and the Sunday homilies at the Cathedral of San Salvador. We remember the unforgettable words he said in an interview with *Excelsior* magazine of Mexico, just two weeks before his death:

I ought to say, that as a Christian, I do not believe in death without resurrection. If they kill me, I will rise again in the people of El Salvador. I'm not boasting; I say it with the greatest humility. I am bound as pastor by a divine command to give my life for those whom I love, and that means all

Salvadorians, even those who are going to kill me. If they manage to carry out their threats, as of now, I offer my blood for the redemption and resurrection of El Salvador. If God accepts the sacrifice of my life, then may my blood be the seed of liberty and the sign that hope will soon become a reality. May my death, if it is accepted by God, be for the liberation of my people, as a witness of hope in what is to come. You call tell them that, if they succeed in killing me, I pardon and bless those who do it. A bishop may die, but the Church of God, which is the people, will never die. Let us end where we began.

Romero is a follower of Jesus Christ. Jesus announced a new commandment—the commandment of love—and went to the extreme of proposing forgiveness for offenses and love of enemies.

Jesus said: "I say to you: love your enemies, do good deeds to those who hate you, pray for those who persecute you so that you shall be children of God."

Romero followed Jesus and forgave his persecutors. He knew how to condemn the sin and save the sinner. The victory of fraternity over violence cannot be assured without forgiveness—the most precious fruit of mercy. The world can only become ever more human when we succeed in introducing forgiveness in all relationships. Forgiveness proves that love exists in the world and it is far more powerful than sin. A bishop may die, but the Church of God will never die. Bishop Romero is alive. How does Bishop Romero live? He is in our midst today. He lives like Jesus—risen from the dead. He is with his people who are seeking and proclaiming the truth freely and resisting manipulation. Those who proclaim the truth live in the spirit testified to by his martyrdom, and they seek a just and peaceful resolution to the present conflict. The spirit is present in so many women and men who live and suffer in our communities today, unknown but moved by the Holy Spirit which inspires new witnesses of truth and love, and which assures us that an end will come to war, to repression, to assassinations, to refugee camps, and to the suffering of so many innocent people. We realize that the death of Romero was not an isolated fact, but part of the witness of the Church which at Medellín and Puebla made a preferential option for the poor.

Bishop Romero's martyrdom helped us understand the reality of our people, a reality of death from hunger and sickness, of uncountable crosses that weigh down our continent, where peasants, shanty dwellers, laborers, students, priests, factory workers, religious, and bishops are jailed, tortured, and killed for believing in Jesus Christ and for loving the poor.

Why does Bishop Romero continue to live? He lives on to do good, to give testimony to a total love for the people. His gospel for us is good news for the world today. Can we do anything? There are many forms of solidarity possible. In the United States several groups are seeking to promote awareness of institutional injustice in Latin America. In this way they are continuing the work of Bishop Oscar Romero by becoming witnesses of love, liberty, and justice among the oppressed of the world.

On 30 March 1980, we bishops present at Bishop Romero's funeral affirmed our commitment to complete his unfinished Mass cut short by bullets. We committed ourselves to carry on his last homily in which he called for an end to all repression, all over the continent and especially in El Salvador. We begged Jesus Christ to give us the grace to be more faithful in our option for the poor and oppressed, to remain firm in the struggle for justice, to be faithful witnesses to God and to his kingdom.

Each Christian is called upon to overcome injustice. This victory shall never be definitively conquered on earth because the mystery of evil will always be present in history. But united in our efforts, always more unified by the spirit of Christ, it will be possible to build a more just and fraternal world. Bishop Romero's life testifies that fraternity can overcome violence, just as love can overcome hatred.

Bishop Oscar Romero was killed. A bishop may die, but the Church of God, which is the people, will never die. Remembrance and reflection is for all of us, and for Romero also, a gift from God.

I invite you to join with me in a little prayer:

In the name of the Father and the Son and the Holy Spirit, we thank you, God, for all the graces and gifts received. At this moment we remember the people of El Salvador, Nicaragua, and all the countries who are suffering and waiting for Christian charity, love, and peace. We know that we are united in faith and hope and we ask you, Father, to bless all our sisters and brothers all over the world. Amen.

3

Monseñor Oscar Romero

Human Rights Apostle

(2000)

ROBERTO CUÉLLAR M.

We were waiting for Monseñor Romero at the cancer clinic, where he lived during his three years as archbishop of San Salvador, but he arrived too late to join our working lunch. We talked by telephone and, for the last time, I heard his voice. It was 3:30 in the afternoon of 24 March 1980. Monseñor Romero had asked me to meet with a high-level delegation from the National Conference of Bishops, the National Council of Churches, and the United States Catholic Conference. His final interview, focusing on the violence then overwhelming El Salvador, was with these same delegates. A few minutes after 6:30 that evening, two nuns from the clinic shouted the news of his assassination through the main door of the Jesuits' Academy in San Salvador. I ran to the building where he had been taken. Just by lifting his left arm, I knew that he was already dead.

Decades later, the confused images of that tragic night return to my mind: ecclesiastical leaders holding urgent meetings; the forensic exam of the archbishop's cadaver; the hundreds of journalists and television cameras; the army, tense and barricaded in the streets; the bombs of the guerrillas; the police investigation of the chapel where Romero had been shot; the sacrificial altar; and above all, the silent parade before his lifeless body of those who had loved him best—the men and women of the most impoverished neighborhoods in San Salvador.

In the ensuing years Monseñor Romero has become a legend for genera-tions of Salvadorans and an icon all over the world. It is still difficult to evalu-ate the effect that his assassination and martyrdom have had on the history of El Salvador and of Central America. Is there peace in Central America? To what extent are our societies more humane? What weight do the fundamen-tal rights of the human person carry today? It is equally difficult to evaluate the effect that this simple, spiritual man's life and example have had on the con-science of Salvadorans and Central Americans. He was greatly loved by many all over the world; and some in my country despised him.

To speak with you today of the fourth archbishop of San Salvador and of his tenacious work in defense of human rights is, for me, a privilege and a chal-lenge. It is, above all, an honor, threatening to overwhelm me.

My life changed radically that day at the end of March 1977 when I, along with several other young lawyers and law students, were introduced to Mon-señor Romero and presented to him as his legal team. I was twenty-four years old at the time, and the archbishop did not seem very convinced at first that this group of young people would be able to give him the legal assistance that the Catholic Church needed.

The group of students and lawyers who met with him that day had been convened only a short time earlier by Father Segundo Montes, a Jesuit priest who was assassinated in El Salvador nine years after Monseñor Romero. Father Montes had brought us together as alumni of the Jesuit Academy to organize a legal service to defend the human rights of the poorest Salvadorans. We called our new organization "Legal Aid" (Socorro Jurídico). The legal services we provided were an expression of social charity, a legal response to the "pref-erential option for the poor" that motivated so many men and women of good-will throughout Latin America during those difficult years of terrorism and military dictatorship.

The man we were to work with, Oscar Romero, had been born in the home of a poor workingman in Ciudad Barrios. He studied in Rome during the Sec-ond World War and then became a priest, well respected throughout the di-oceses in the eastern part of the country. After serving briefly as bishop of Santiago de Maria, Father Romero was appointed archbishop of San Salvador in 1977. In a turbulent time, he seemed the perfect successor—one who would not rock the boat. But shortly after he assumed his new office several priests, including one of his closest associates, were assassinated, the victims of esca-lating violence and intolerance. During his first months as archbishop, Romero's agenda was dictated by urgent necessities and brutal acts of repression directed against the Catholic Church.

The formation of Legal Aid marked the first time in history that a Central American church appeared before the courts to represent the destitute. Our work was a legal response to the Beatitudes, inspired by the social doctrine of the church. "Aid," as Monseñor Romero affectionately referred to us in his homilies, stood up for the poor and defended their human rights during an exceedingly violent period in the history of El Salvador.

The young lawyers of Legal Aid met with the archbishop that afternoon in 1977 in response to Romero's search for lawyers who would defend the interests of the Church after the assassination of the Jesuit priest Rutilio Grande. Father Grande, respected by all of the bishops, had been machine-gunned to death on 12 March 1977 in the town of Aguilares. We represented the archbishop before various judges in a trial that did nothing to clarify the crime and which gave the murderers impunity. Nevertheless, that meeting changed the history of Legal Aid and the lives of many of its lawyers. Without a doubt, it radically changed my life. From that day until his death in 1980, I served the archbishop faithfully, directing legal services and the defense of human rights for the Office of the Archbishop in San Salvador.

From the beginning of his appointment as archbishop, Monseñor Romero recognized the value and importance of having an honest team of lawyers that the Church could consult on legal matters. After he took office, we began to see a parade of victims filing through the offices of Legal Aid. The vast majority was poor, but there were also persons from other social classes who had economic resources but could not find lawyers who would defend them because of their ideas and activities.

In El Salvador in the time of Monseñor Romero it was commonplace—a habitual daily occurrence—for persons to be detained without cause, to be punished under emergency legislation and national security laws, to be given no opportunity to defend themselves against their accusers, to be assassinated because of their ideas, to be tortured in clandestine prisons, to be kidnapped, and to be "disappeared."

Within this tragic scenario, Monseñor Romero became an apostle for human rights—a cause in which he can be considered an authentic pioneer. He undertook continuous strategic efforts to develop a human rights policy and ministry. He always did what was needed and did it when it needed to be done. He was always in the right place at the right time with love, courage, and moral strength, as a true follower of the Gospel. In this way he was able, within a very short time, to develop a creative and wide-ranging trajectory of active defense and lucid teachings on the rights that adhere to the human person.

In the highly ideological and polarized time period in which the archbishop lived, he saw the relationship between individual human rights abuses and systemic violence. From common law came political law. From legal representation came international denunciation. From local inquiries came the scrupulous investigation of violations of the national Constitution and of the dignity of the Salvadoran people, to which the archbishop drew public attention Sunday after Sunday.

Monseñor Romero was, in fact, the first human rights ombudsman in the history of El Salvador and its people. He was an ombudsman who knew how to combine the ethics and truth of the Gospel with legal defense and public denunciation. He was an ombudsman who sought, in the limited legal framework available, some means to promote democracy and one who always made use of solidarity and justice in his ministry of accompaniment. He was a human rights ombudsman fundamentally inspired by the Beatitudes: give food to the hungry, provide drink to the thirsty, console the brokenhearted, and visit those who are in prison. This was the law by which he lived. I remember how frequently he repeated the parable of the Good Samaritan. In acting as he did, Monseñor Romero bound the vast majority of Salvadorans together in the cause of human rights. No one before him had been able to do this in El Salvador. Nor has anyone since him done it as effectively as he did during those tumultuous years preceding the outbreak of war.

The soul of public international law and the doctrine of human rights is that states should behave with compassion and mercy toward their own citizens and also toward foreigners. This has been its inspiration from the times of Vitoria and de Suarez. This is what all modern thinkers on public international law have continued to proclaim. Similarly, it was compassion and mercy that inspired and animated all of Monseñor Romero's humanitarian activities.

It is worth pointing out that Monseñor Romero began to use the general principles of law and the doctrine of human rights at a time when international conventions and pacts were still few in number and adequate international human rights legislation did not yet exist. I can still recall his immense joy when, around the middle of 1979, the American Convention on Human Rights entered into effect. Today, when we are saturated with pacts, treaties, and conventions, much of the official discourse has converted these important instruments of justice into abstract papers far removed from those majorities whom they should serve—and whom Monseñor Romero approached directly in order to serve.

From his position, Monseñor Romero promoted all of the rights of all citizens on the basis of two fundamental principles: everyone deserves protection because no one in El Salvador is secure, even in something as basic as his or her own life; and everyone needs protection because the vast majorities are legally disenfranchised. Deserving humanitarian protection and needing legal protection were the two pillars on which he oriented his human rights practice.

He never privileged anyone, and he was consistent from beginning to end in his message: access to justice for all, without discrimination for reasons of social class, religion, gender, or viewpoint.

In the history of humankind, Monseñor Romero holds a place among the great defenders of human rights, both for his theory and for his practice. His influence is Salvadoran, Central American, and global. While he was alive his voice was heard around the world, and his Sunday homilies, proclaimed from the Cathedral of San Salvador—his "bench" as archbishop—turned him into an international paradigm for the promotion and defense of human rights. Each Sunday he would spend more than an hour on theological themes, interpreting the readings from that week's liturgy and delivering a message of reconciliation to a society bloodied and divided by violence. He would then dedicate as much time as was needed to narrate the most important events that had taken place that week. In that "spoken Sunday newspaper" he reported what the national media—controlled and censored by an authoritarian and repressive state—could not report. And his message was broadcast through the Church's own means of mass communication, the Catholic weekly *Orientación* and, especially, the radio station YSAX, both of which were dynamited on many occasions by death squads and paramilitary groups.

Many of the events that Oscar Romero revealed in his homilies were grave human rights violations directed against the poorest Salvadorans. That an archbishop would publicly relate these deeds, often in great detail, resulted in something unprecedented. His was not a calculated gesture; it was his compassionate and indignant response to the national reality. It was the response of a humanist, a democrat, and a Christian. And, of course, there were very few who dared to make such a public response in the dangerous El Salvador of those years.

Monseñor Romero's emphasis on denouncing human rights violations impacted the national community and awoke the interest of the international community, especially those organizations specialized in the defense, promotion, and protection of human rights. In 1978 the International Federation for Human Rights arrived in El Salvador, drawn by Monseñor Romero's denunciations. The Interamerican Commission on Human Rights visited El Salvador in 1979, attracted by the voice of Monseñor Romero. Amnesty International chose El Salvador as its destination for its first large-scale mission to Central America because of Monseñor Romero. From Geneva, the International Commission of Jurists, dedicated to promoting the rule of law and justice throughout the world, visited El Salvador to listen to the archbishop. A congressional delegation from the United States made its first investigation of human rights violations, motivated by the courageous words proclaimed each Sunday by Monseñor Romero from the cathedral. Also from Geneva, the Protestant churches and other Christian denominations united in the World Council of Churches encouraged its Commission on International Concerns to accompany Archbishop Romero in his work. Shortly before his assassination, the British Parliament presented Monseñor Romero as its nominee for the Nobel Peace Prize.

Monseñor Romero, who was the best jurist among all of the lawyers who worked with him, young or old, also knew how to expose the vice and corruption of El Salvador's judicial system. He was a man of laws. His orthodox and conservative formation led him to the conviction that it was possible to confront social problems by changing the laws, making them inclusive and struggling so that judicial alternatives would not be closed to the cry for justice of the most impoverished Salvadorans.

From this legal but not legalistic perspective, based on respect and appreciation for the law, Romero provided a constitutional framework for the defense of those human rights that were being violated on a daily basis by the Salvadoran power structure. Using this perspective, he repeatedly pointed to the corruption of the law in El Salvador and emphasized the dangers that existed because the laws were not an expression of what they should be under "Just Law," a concept he referred to in many homilies in order to remind governments of what they had forgotten or—as in the case in El Salvador at that time—of what they had never learned: that the legitimate power to make laws, to legislate, belongs only to those who exercise it via the delegation of a sovereign people.

The fact that this had not happened in our country created an urgent need to work for the full development of persons until they could become sovereign creators of their own destiny. The law, said he, derives its power in the final analysis from the allegiance that the vast majority of citizens give to those who apply it. This was one of the ideas he asserted with great persistence and force.

With his word Monseñor Romero battled the unjust laws that were imposed on the majority of citizens through brute force. Often the human damage that these laws caused was understood only when the archbishop explained it in his homilies. Using concrete cases, he called attention to unjust penal processes, explained how prisoners had faced corrupt judges, and detailed the confrontation of some victims with military judges wielding extensive coercive powers.

Frequently he discussed the process of creating law and how this process had been corrupted. On many occasions I saw him scrutinizing the laws, analyzing them. He studied the Constitution; he studied the Penal Code; he studied the repressive laws related to national security, such as the infamous Law of Defense and Guarantee of the Public Order, the source of so much damage and pain. And, in the midst of that political convulsion, the archbishop always proposed legal exits, pushing us onward whenever we were tempted to use judicial principles and legal precepts to ensnare ourselves. Monseñor Romero was a true jurist.

His homilies were, therefore, an extraordinary education—free and open to the public—on political rights, civil rights, and the critique of repressive laws. His homily on Pentecost, 14 May 1978, was especially famous and a key to his pastoral ministry. On that occasion he responded to the Supreme Court's demand that he reveal the names of the "corrupt judges" he had referred to in a previous homily—a demand that constituted a dangerous political trap. To respond to the Court he undertook a detailed study of the laws and Constitution which convinced him, once and for all, that the best way to defend the fundamental rights of those who had nothing and who could count on nothing except for the power of his voice in the cathedral was to engage in a profound interpretation of the only legal tool that counted inside El Salvador, the Political Constitution, and the only helpful legal tool that then existed outside of El Salvador, the Universal Declaration of Human Rights.

At that time El Salvador had neither signed a single human rights convention nor accepted any international obligation to respond to human rights violations. International humanitarian law was unknown in the country, and the American Convention was not recognized until very shortly before the archbishop's assassination. Human rights protection, which is today an international judicial discipline, did not exist in his time, either in fruit or in bud.

Although people spoke of the need to protect human rights, the term "human rights protection" had not yet been given precise juridical meaning. Monseñor Romero told me that for him, as a common man, the Bible and the Constitution were the two sacred codes by which he lived. Whenever we confronted a judicial problem, he always asked me, "What does the Constitution say to protect this person?" And I usually replied, "It doesn't say anything, Monseñor. The Constitution doesn't apply in this country."

He often questioned the attitude of lawyers, including those of us who had the enormous good fortune of working closely with him. When he noticed us becoming pessimistic and showing little inclination to make use of constitutional law, he insisted: "We look to what it says to see what we can do." And with his tenacious searching he always managed to find some light. In this way he was giving life, under the most difficult circumstances imaginable, to an expression as vague and diffuse as "the legal protection of human rights." In several of his homilies the archbishop called upon the courts and the judges, imploring them to comply with the Constitution, which stated that no person was to be deprived of life, liberty, or property without due process. This precept, with a clear meaning under the law, was also a measure of human rights protection.

To this constitutional precept he added several other principles of due process, including the presumption of innocence until guilt is proven, and the injunction against ex post facto laws. Monseñor Romero urged us to argue the unconstitutionality of some laws, to use habeas corpus laws to demand the exhibition of detainees, and to utilize all administrative protections. He was convinced that the Constitution contained tools to remedy the constant violation of fundamental rights. This conviction turned him into a pioneer because a major premise of modern constitutional law is that the Constitution should possess the means to confront violations to itself in the form of human rights abuses. He always told us: insist on justice and use the law, even when laws are not fulfilled and some are unjust.

By acting this way, Romero offered us and the precarious Salvadoran legal community a great opportunity to use human rights to think about the legal corruption that existed in El Salvador and to reflect on the philosophical bases of modern democracies and the living law. He believed that the law could not be reduced to a body of normative rules designed to preserve a blind, static order favoring the interests of the historically privileged classes and closed to the cries of those who needed justice the most. He sought a living law and in human rights he found the best road. He lowered the lofty precepts of human rights to the level of social reality and gave them real content in a way that few in Central America have done in the twenty years since then.

Monseñor Romero was also convinced that the law could be used to promote social and economic justice, even though the constraints of his times meant that his actions were consistently reduced to promoting the rights of individuals, those facing arbitrary judges or military courts, those who had been forcibly disappeared to clandestine police cells, and even those kidnapped by pre-guerrilla groups.

Oscar Romero demonstrated that there was no case of human rights whose principal elements could not be explained simply, putting them within the reach of the people, so that they could be understood by those who had not been technically trained in this material. With his word, in his homilies, and by his actions, Oscar Romero communicated human rights. For him the law was required to offer protection of the rights existing in the Constitution and in the Universal Declaration of Human Rights. It did not need to be abstract or complex.

He maintained that there should be democratic mechanisms for creating new laws or for modifying existing laws when circumstances demanded.

When the Agrarian Reform Act was passed in February 1980, Monseñor Romero spoke of the need for Salvadoran society to use democratic means of reflection to make the law evolve until society could succeed in creating and extending the reach of human rights. Few have understood as he did that the law should be subject to revision and that the rights existing in the Constitution should not only be protected but also reinterpreted and reformed as needed.

It is also important to note that in the many cases of kidnappings in which it fell to Romero to act as intermediary he always insisted that one could not legitimately kidnap others in order to demand the release of persons disappeared by governmental forces—that an evil act could not be used to demand a good. He wanted to avoid that war. He frequently stated that by putting the law before force and making the laws evolve it was possible to create an orderly and peaceful alternative in El Salvador, capable of solving our most serious problems.

Some persons accused the archbishop of instigating trouble, but in truth he exhibited a profound respect toward even his most bloodthirsty critics and had a great talent for skillful mediation and persuasive conciliation. Monseñor Romero always prioritized dialogue, conciliation, communication between opponents, and he always emphasized mediation—from the Christian point of view and from the point of view of the law. I remember the violent strikes of the Santa Ana textile workers and at La Constancia Brewery. I also remember the many Acts of Conciliation signed in the offices of the archbishop that ended those strikes, all inspired by Romero's peaceful words. All the mediations that produced historic results during that turbulent period of violent occupations of churches and industrial properties carried Romero's personal stamp.

I hope that some day we may recover all of those acts and documents for the historical memory of the theory of alternative means of resolving conflict. We must recover, as well, the more than three hundred letters that have been preserved from those that Romero sent to us at the Legal Aid offices, recommending to us each case. His work in human rights was oriented by the idea that just denunciations could only be formulated through the most rigorous investigation of the facts in each and every case, and this is what he did. He concerned himself with each case. He received the people; he personally wrote the letters asking us to attend to this case or that; he argued the case; he suggested that we bring it to the tribunals; and he explained to us in detail why he thought one way or another. His personal touch appears in all of the work done by Legal Aid in those years.

Monseñor Romero was also a victim of human rights violations, and not only because they took his life, assassinating him at the altar when no one else dared to beg, plead, and demand, "In the name of God and this suffering people, stop the repression!"

In a country as violent as El Salvador, Oscar Romero found the time to reflect on the role of law in a society that suffered from drastic and rapid changes and on the consequences that a just and fairly applied law could have in the democratic future that he aspired to and preached. He aspired to a very simple democracy. He often told me that he wanted El Salvador to know "better times" and for it to enjoy at least 30 percent of the democratic guarantees that existed in Costa Rica, a neighboring country that he knew from participating in the meetings of Central American bishops. He directed me to look at the Costa Rican reality, for which he felt a healthy envy: a country without an army; a country with an elevated level of investment in the education of its people, a more equal distribution of its riches, a health plan that might be minimal but which covered the entire population; a country with a free and clean electoral process where vote tallies were respected.

Dignity and equality were the principles that guided Monseñor Romero; he envisioned a legal system based in the sovereign power of the people delegated to representatives legislating for the common good. All of these principles were difficult to reconcile with Salvadoran reality. Yet, using these moral precepts, Monseñor Romero put into movement a very simple and popular method for the defense, protection, and promotion of human rights. It was the first time in Central America that a Church authority utilized the pulpit to present in simple terms the significance of the human rights violations perpetrated against the poor and to clearly promote the legal defense of human rights.

To help him on this path, which he pioneered in Central America, Monseñor Romero turned to Chile's Vicariate of Solidarity. The Vicariate and Legal Aid were born at nearly the same time during similarly difficult periods in the history of the two fraternal nations. Monseñor Romero and Cardinal Raúl Silva Henríquez spoke frequently, creating and refining a similar human rights ministry.

These two pastors were the most significant proponents of their cause in Latin America during that period, with the common denominator that neither of them, and neither of the two institutions they represented, was satisfied with making simple denunciations. Both the Vicariate in Chile and Legal Aid in El Salvador gave legal backing to the prophetic denunciations their pastors made from the pulpit.

Among his other deeds, Monseñor Romero was a pioneer in the humanitarian treatment of internally displaced persons—those peasant families who had fled to the capital as a result of the fighting and repression unleashed with particular fury in the countryside. Toward the end of his life Monseñor Romero set up Latin America's first refugee camps for internally displaced persons, in the San José de la Montana Seminary in San Salvador and later in the basilica. This was the first time that the Salvadoran Catholic Church had opened its doors to shelter those displaced by a warlike conflict. It was the first time in Latin America that internally displaced persons were the subjects of humanitarian protection.

The Cartagena Declaration on Refugees and Displaced Persons took effect years after Romero opened the first refuge in San Salvador. This intervention, like the rest of his humanitarian work, was born from his faith, mercy, and compassion. In this his message and his teachings, as well as his methods, are universal and continue to be relevant all these years after his death.

Monseñor Romero's message continues to be valid. If he were to speak to the development agencies, humanitarian organizations, and human rights groups that exist today, he would tell them to give effective and efficient service to the poor—who continue to be the majority in Latin America and who are a substantial and increasing minority even in the United States. Speaking to us today, Romero would say that human rights are violated not only in warfare but also in democracies whenever corruption, favoritism, injustice, and lack of social consciousness predominate. As a prophet and as a martyr, Oscar Romero is the most important figure in recent Christian history.

Three days after Romero's death, when we were preparing his death certificate for the funeral to be held on 30 March 1980, two employees from San Salvador's municipal offices and a street negotiator of the type who always gather around public spaces in Central America said to me, in unison, "Could it be that we are about to bury a saint?" At that painful moment I could not assimilate the idea, which had already begun to be shared by many Salvadorans. Today, this is certain: that from the first instant that followed his tragic and glorious death Monseñor Romero entered into the heart of our country's history, transforming himself into the one who most stands out in our collective memory as the Salvadoran to enter Heaven by the Great Gate at the end of the twentieth century.

Today, so many years after that fateful day, I have not been able to forget. Nor will I ever forget the three years I worked with him, years in which I received from him and his example a priceless inheritance. Today, so many years later, I reflect on the developments in international human rights protection that took place after Romero's death, inspired by his words—developments before the Interamerican Commission for Human Rights and the various human rights organs of the United Nations, developments that we continued to advance from exile on behalf of Salvadorans until 1987.

In the years since Romero's death I have engaged in many other works, some of them internationally significant. Since 15 October 1999, I have served as director of the Interamerican Institute for Human Rights, an important position for the protection of human rights. Nevertheless, neither this nor any other work that I have done since Archbishop Romero's death—nor that I believe I am likely to do in the future—do I consider to be so profound in its teachings, so beautiful in its solidarity, and so important for human rights as the three years that I lived immersed in the humanitarian ministry of the fourth archbishop of San Salvador.

No other mission has given me such honor or satisfaction as accompanying in the defense of human rights that good man who became a martyr for his people and will soon be honored as a saint, my fellow Salvadoran, Oscar Romero.

4

The Empowering Spirit of Archbishop Romero

A Personal Testimony

(1995)

RUBÉN ZAMORA

On 24 March 1980, Archbishop Romero was shot to death and today we are probably killing him again. Still, the empowering spirit of Romero might be communicated to a new generation of men and women who were only children when Romero's prophetic words—"Cease the repression!"—echoed across the radio waves of El Salvador. Today, thanks to a historic peace accord, the brutal political violence of the 1970s and '80s has subsided. However, to simply repeat Romero's critique of repression in this context may be to let his words fall deafly on our times.

To keep his spirit alive, we should bear in mind the transformation which Romero himself underwent. Although often characterized as a sudden, radical conversion from cleric to prophet, the change in his relationship with the people of El Salvador was gradual. From the beginning of his service to the San Miguel Diocese, an assignment which was to last twenty-two years, Romero was sensitive to the plight of the poor who form the vast majority of Salvadoran society. He gave shelter to drunken persons on the street and asked the wealthy for money, which he would redistribute to the hungry. However, this was only an "external" relationship to poverty.

All of that changed when Romero became the bishop of Santiago de Maria and began to know the poor not simply as beggars in the street but as working people struggling to survive inhuman conditions. His diocese was flooded every year during the coffee-picking season with peasants who came from all over the country to work in the *cafetales,* and who, after a hard day's labor, would have to sleep on the ground. Appalled, Romero provided them with shelter in empty seminary buildings and began to wonder how the owners of the coffee *fincas*—Christian families who would go to church on Sundays and partake of the Eucharist—could treat their workers in such a manner. These reflections led him to examine the structural roots of poverty.

Romero was also moved by a massacre in his diocese in July of 1975. He visited the scene, and the brutalized and tortured bodies he saw led him to write a confidential letter to President Molina denouncing the practices of the security forces. Nevertheless, he remained unwilling to take a public stand on behalf of the poor.

Finally, the National Guard's assassination of one of the priests of his diocese, Fr. Rutilio Grande, completed the transformation of Romero from a giver of charity to a vocal advocate of justice. He no longer saw the poor merely as objects of compassion, but as persons and as agents of change. Though a quiet man, his voice seemed to swell with strength at Mass on Sunday when he would publicly denounce injustice and violence, willingly confronting the government and the military. In one Sunday homily he adamantly critiqued the corruption in the judicial system. Members of the judiciary followed on Monday with a full-page ad in the newspaper denouncing Romero and demanding that he produce evidence for his accusations. I was among the lawyers who subsequently counseled Romero that he stood no chance in court against the court itself, and we advised him to drop the issue in the hope that it would die away. The following Sunday, I listened with extra attentiveness to the archbishop's weekly radio homily and gasped in disbelief as Romero followed his usual lengthy theological exposition with another attack on the judicial corruption.

How can this voice, which challenged the war-torn El Salvador of the 1970s with the hope and vision of the Gospel of Jesus Christ, be a transforming influence yet today? I believe the significance of Romero's life does transcend the particular historical configurations of his era, and I suggest to you three ways in which his spirit might continue to empower El Salvador.

First, the transformation in Romero's relationship to the poor is a testimony to the importance of attending to the structural and social roots of poverty. Thankfully, the political violence in El Salvador has subsided. The peace accord is a fundamental reordering of the Salvadoran public, but—as important as it is—it is only the beginning of the changes the society must undergo. It does not begin to address the economic problems of the country, which now clamor for attention. The trend towards absolutization of the market does not prioritize the provision of bread and basic goods to the majority of the Salvadoran people, and it threatens the persistence of material and cultural poverty. My feeling would be that Romero would not like neoliberal economics.

Romero's life also speaks to us today by virtue of the archbishop's tireless call for dialogue and negotiation. In a society that was terribly polarized, a society in which the usual way to relate to persons with whom one disagreed was to assassinate them, Romero always tried to open a space for communication, conversation, and understanding. In 1980, for example, as an attempt at co-governance by military and civilian leaders was about to disintegrate, Romero brought the opposing sides together for four hours of talks, urging that the junta be given another chance. His example of bridgebuilding can be of particular importance to an El Salvador in which political change is often seen as a process of flipping over the tortilla, so that those on the bottom of society take the place of those on top. Romero's life suggests a different model of societal transformation. As El Salvador enters a critical juncture in the peace process as U.N. observers prepare to leave and those disgruntled by the accord's outcome may be tempted again to engage in violence, Romero's plea for forgiveness and reconciliation is of paramount significance.

Lastly, Romero can inspire by the manner in which he brought together Christianity and politics. Drawing on Pius XII's theology of the mystical body of Christ, Vatican II's *Gaudium et Spes*, and his own living relationship with the Salvadoran people, Romero testified that the church must be the voice of the voiceless and the incessant defender of life. The church must passionately pursue justice—but without identifying itself with any one particular party or any one particular ideology. This can be a very difficult struggle, as the entries in Romero's diary suggest. To walk this tightrope was especially challenging in the El Salvador of the 1970s, which was so highly politicized that people were often not seen as persons but instead were identified only on the basis of their membership in political organizations. In this context, I remember that Romero always asked me when I arrived to discuss politics, "How are your children? How is your wife?" And while he tirelessly defended the right of the poor to organize, he was very critical of popular organizations which became overly or one-sidedly political. His wariness of politicization is especially important to El Salvador today, I believe, as the country struggles to move from being a narrowly political society to being a civil community. The testimony of the life of Oscar Romero—a man who addressed the structural roots of poverty and related to the poor as persons, a man who incessantly sought forgiveness and reconciliation, a man who gave his life because he believed both that Christ impels us to seek justice and that our ultimate liberation is not of this world—can thus be reinterpreted for our times. If we fail to do so, we risk transforming the living reality of Romero into a statue.

"Beloved young people," Romero said in a homily in 1978, "the older generation (my own, I regret) is leaving you a heritage of so much selfishness, of so much evil." The living reality of the martyred archbishop is itself, in contrast, a legacy of compassionate goodness, love in the face of hatred, hope in the face of terrible suffering, deep faith, and homiletic words which can indeed still challenge us today: "Renew, new wheat, newly sown crops, fields still fresh from God's hand. Children, youths: be a better world."

5

Archbishop Romero and His Commitment to the Church
(1999)

MARGARET SWEDISH

It is important that we reflect on the commitment of Archbishop Oscar Romero to the institutional Church for several reasons. First, because we cannot understand the prophetic role of Monsignor Romero or his pastoral commitment without understanding his commitment to the institution of the Church as specifically expressed in his leadership of the Archdiocese of San Salvador. One of the most significant aspects of his brief tenure as pastor of the archdiocese is the manner in which the institution and the prophetic and pastoral works of the Church became one, became integrated, flowed into each other. The institution was molded to be of service to its mission, and that mission was forged by the history in which Romero and his pastoral workers found themselves: a situation of political violence and military repression that was savage in its expression within a context of inhuman poverty and extremes of injustice and social and economic disparity.

This implied a shift on many levels—in the *óptica*, or perspective/vantage point, from which the Church viewed its historical reality; in its understanding of power and Church authority and how these are exercised in the world; in organizational structures and structures of decisionmaking; in the role of the Church within the sociopolitical reality of El Salvador at that time; in the Church's stance in the face of that reality; and in the content of the word that it preached.

Second, this reflection is important because Romero presented a challenge of profound importance to the "universal" Church, a challenge whose full implications I believe we have only begun to fully appreciate. It is a challenge that emerged from the Latin American Church in the 1970s and one that was crystallized for many of us in the witness of this great martyr of our hemisphere. It is a challenge for the Church everywhere—to ask itself what this institution is created to be, what its purpose is in the history in which it carries out its gospel mission.

It is a challenge to look at the institution in the historical context of our changing times and to put that Church constantly, in an ever-flowing and evolving manner, at the service of the reign of God. That means being willing to look honestly at the world and to immerse the Church into the world—the challenge of the Second Vatican Council and, of great importance to Romero, the challenge of the Latin American Bishops Conference (CELAM) in its historic gathering at Medellín, Colombia, in 1968.

Third, it is important to reflect on this topic because what Romero did in putting his archdiocese at the service of God's people in a time of terrible persecution and violence revitalized the Church of El Salvador. Overflowing crowds attended his Masses at the cathedral; there were record numbers of vocations; hundreds of catechists and Delegates of the Word were trained to lead and animate the growing numbers of base communities; and millions of people throughout Latin America listened to his homilies on the archdiocesan radio station, YSAX.

The bishop understood the concept of pastor as a "good shepherd" in a real gospel sense, as one who shared a word that ignited faith in the hearts of his hearers. The institutional leader embodied, both in his role as bishop and in the structures of the archdiocese, a word that his people recognized as the authentic reflection of their own truth. The institution was put at the service of this truth. The result was a flourishing and vibrant Church, willing to follow Jesus even to death on the cross.

This is amazing, if we really absorb it. It may be hard for us, coming out of our relatively comfortable North American reality, to fully appreciate this commitment on the part of thousands of Christians—priests, religious, catechists, Delegates of the Word, and base community leaders and members—anxious to follow this Jesus, persecuted and crucified, in the context of truly encountering the gospel in the Church of the Archdiocese of San Salvador, even if it meant following him to death.

So I want to explore these themes and see how they challenge us here today, call us to follow an example with truly "universal" implications for us and for our Church. To truly appreciate how Romero molded his institution to the service of its gospel mission, we must understand how he understood "Church." For him the Church was a living, breathing "space" in which the building of the reign of God was taking place. It was not a static reality but rather a constantly evolving reality being molded and shaped by the same history that is the subject of God's saving action. The institution, then, as the organized structure of the Church, was also not to be static. It was to be a "body" of human beings of faith constantly attentive to how God is acting in the world to bring about that reign.

In his second pastoral letter, written for the great Salvadoran feast of the Transfiguration, 6 August 1977, Romero articulates this vision of "Church." The letter is entitled "The Church, the Body of Christ in History." The title is revelatory of his vision.

Romero writes in this letter that "the Church's foundation is not to be thought of in a legal or juridical sense, as if Christ gathered some persons together, entrusted them with a teaching, gave them a kind of constitution, but then himself remained apart from them." It is not this kind of static universality that Christ intended, a static truth entrusted to an inflexible, unchanging organizational structure. A narrow concept of Church, Romero believed, killed the spirit; it did not allow for the action of God in history, the continuing unfolding of the history of redemption through the body of Christ which is the Church. Thus, Romero writes, "Christ founded his Church so that he himself could go on being present in the history of humanity precisely through the group of Christians who make up his Church. The Church is the flesh in which Christ makes present down the ages his own life and his personal mission."

The Church is flesh. It is testimony to God's incarnation—God taking on our humanity, coming into our history and sharing our destiny with us:

> The Church can be Church only so long as it goes on being the Body of Christ. Its mission will be authentic only so long as it is the mission of Jesus in the new situations, the new circumstances, of history. The criterion

that will guide the Church will be neither the approval of, nor the fear of, men and women, no matter how powerful or threatening they may be. It is the Church's duty in history to lend its voice to Christ so that he may speak, its feet so that he may walk today's world, its hands to build the kingdom, and to offer all its members "to make up all that has still to be undergone by Christ." (Col. 1:24)[1]

The Church, Romero says in this pastoral letter, "is a community of faith whose primary obligation, whose raison d'être, is to tirelessly continue the life and work of Jesus. . . . [It] principally exists for the evangelization of the human race. Yes, it is an institution; it is made up of persons; and it has forms and structures. But all that is for a much more basic reality: the exercise of its task of evangelization."

When the Church does this, when it continues, "in the course of history, the work that Jesus carried out," then it is truly "the Body of Christ in history."[2] Jesus, Romero reminds us, "fulfilled his mission in a particular kind of world, in a particular sort of society. Like him, the Church does not simply proclaim the reign of God in the abstract. It also has to promote "the solutions that seem most likely to bring the kingdom into being, that are most just."[3]

The word is not static; the body of Christ cannot live within a static institution. It lives in history and is shaped by that history. If it is not, if it tries to remain outside history—"above" it, if you will—concentrating only on the transcendent reality of God, it will have little authentic to say to history, no substantial word of denunciation of sin within it or of the redemption taking place through it. The Church's role, as it models the example of Jesus, is to live immersed in its world and to speak to its particular reality, as Jesus did. It is to proclaim the reign of God within the particularity of that history and to create a space in which the action of God-saving-us-in-history can be carried out.

The Church, its structures, its pastoral leaders, all of its members, and all the community of believers must be involved in creating that space and in being active agents of God's saving action. It is precisely here that the prophetic witness of Oscar Romero is fully integrated with the institutional Church he led, for he put his Church at the service of this saving action of God, of Jesus Christ still present and active in history.

This commitment to put his Church at the service of the history of salvation meant a Church on the move, a Church that can change according to the new challenges it confronts in history, a Church evolving, a pilgrim Church. In his fourth pastoral letter, "The Church's Mission amid the National Crisis," written for 6 August 1979, Romero reflects on two essential aspects of the Church's mission: the gospel message we preach, and the changing reality of peoples, times, and places in which the Church finds itself and where it has to fulfill its mission. He challenges the Church to "shake off our laziness and bring ourselves up to date," to use every means available to help us understand the real situation in which we find ourselves, and—here he quotes from the CELAM conference at Puebla, Mexico, in January 1979—"to adapt the gospel message to today's human beings in a dynamic, attractive, and convincing way."[4]

He adds: "In this attitude of search, let us recall that the Church is historical, that it is moving forward. It is not something fixed and determined. It does not have a closed system for interpreting the gospel, applicable to each epoch and to every circumstance. The Church is a pilgrim. The word of God is inexhaustible; it forever discloses new facets that have to be more deeply understood. So the Church goes on evolving in the way it presents the unique message of the gospel, in keeping with the particular period in which it is living."

"We believe in the Lord of history, and in his Spirit who makes all things new." Echoing the words of Pope Paul VI in his encyclical, *On Evangelization in the Modern World* (9, 30), Romero reflected that the Church is challenged to preach a "liberating evangelization." In posing the question of what evangelization the Church should offer El Salvador, he expressed his firm faith that through the Church's evangelization "the full force for liberation with which our divine Redeemer has endowed [the Church] may run its course."[5]

This, then, is the space that he sought to create within the institution of his archdiocese, of his Church—a space where the full force of God's liberation may run its course. I continue to be moved and awed by the faith of this man in the God of history and the enormity of his hope that the Church could rise to such a challenge.

Yet, in all he wrote and preached, Romero stood on the firm ground of the Church's doctrine, its deposit of faith, and its social teachings. He quoted Pope Paul VI often and referred repeatedly to the Vatican Council, to Medellín, and to Puebla. He said over and over that what he sought to do, simply, was to make real in the Archdiocese of San Salvador the teachings handed down through these important channels. He cited especially Pope Paul's encyclical as the pastoral model that he was implementing in his archdiocese. Maybe this is what is so astounding: that Archbishop Romero, believing that the social teaching of the Church was fundamental to its identity, sought to embrace it not just in word and teaching, in pastoral letters or official Church statements that no one reads or puts into practice, but in the very institutional structures of his archdiocese—even when that meant the risk of persecution for the faith. Where else have we seen anything like it? He brought together all the dynamism of the original gospel story within the urgency of his moment in the history of El Salvador and wedded his institutional Church to that force for life. The Church and the gospel were truly one.

And he did this as archbishop, as a member of the hierarchy. He saw the archbishop's role and the Church's role as a servant of the suffering people. The liberating gospel, the announcement of God's redeeming action in history, was being revealed through the journey of cross and resurrection of the Salvadoran people; therefore, the Church had to go there, to the suffering people, to hear and to announce this good news. This had important implications for the institutions of the Church, for the hierarchy, for pastoral workers, for catechesis, for sacramental ministries, for religious training—in other words, for how the institution organized itself to reflect this dynamic call to follow Jesus into the world. It meant taking on an attitude of humility—not just personally but institutionally—in order to listen to history through the voices of those marginalized, oppressed, and repressed—a humility that allowed those voices to change him, to affect his role as archbishop, to influence the word he spoke, and to help shape that space in which the full force of God's liberating action could run its course.

The result was a Church fiercely relevant and alive, at the service of its people, a voice so authentic that its message was immediately recognized, both when it denounced sin and when it announced the good news to the poor, when it announced the coming of salvation into the world, and when it defined the way it was coming about. That, of course, is why he was so loved—and so hated. As with the case of Jesus of Nazareth, salvation was not a neutral word.

This commitment to total honesty with history, with the conditions that existed in his country, and to bringing the light of the gospel to that history, implied a shift in orientation for the Church of El Salvador. As in much of Latin America, the Salvadoran Church had been historically tied to the economic and political elites. Church leaders appeared at inaugurations of military dictators to bless their regimes. Romero was the first to refuse to do so, and this after the murder of Fr. Rutilio Grande, S.J., just weeks after Romero's installation as archbishop.

But when Romero looked at his world of El Salvador and saw there, as he described so eloquently in his famous address at Louvain University on 2 February 1980, "the real faces of the poor, about which Puebla speaks: the land-workers living in misery, factory workers who have no labor rights . . . human beings who are at the mercy of cold economic calculations . . . the mothers and the wives of those who have disappeared or who are political prisoners . . . the shantytown dwellers, whose wretchedness defies the imagination, suffering the permanent mockery of the nearby mansions. [It is] within this world devoid of human face, this contemporary sacrament of the suffering servant of Yahweh, that the Church of my archdiocese has undertaken to incarnate itself."[6]

In other words, this encounter with the poor of El Salvador meant a shift in the position of the Church within that history. It meant breaking with structures of sin that cause this massive human suffering, this defacing of the image of God in the human person. This incarnation is not an action that comes from outside the world but rather from within it, modeling the incarnation of the gospel. Following Jesus' action, this Church goes close to the world of the poor, the ones who are suffering the inhuman violation of their dignity, a dignity made sacred not only by the incarnation but in God's very act of creation when the human being was made in the image of God. It goes to the outcast, the Samaritans, the lepers, the prostitutes, and the tax collectors, and from there it searches for the truth of how God is acting in history to redeem this situation and to liberate the human person.

And so Romero took his Church to this world devoid of human face—in this case the peasants, the factory workers, the unemployed, the outcast and marginalized, the tortured, and the families of the disappeared. He let the implications of his vantage point change the orientation of his Church, its institutional structures, the mission of service to its people.

His vision was at once simple and profound: "This coming closer to the world of the poor is what we understand both by the incarnation and by conversion. The changes that were needed within the Church and in its apostate, in education, in religious and priestly life, in lay movements, which we had not brought about simply by looking inward upon the Church, we are now carrying out by turning ourselves outward toward the world of the poor."[7]

In this way and from this vantage point, "the Church makes its option for the poor—for the truly poor, not for the fictitiously poor . . . for those who are really oppressed and repressed"[8]—an option made from within history, within the society in which the poor find themselves, within a necessarily political reality formed by structures that shape and enforce a situation of sin reflected in the violation of the dignity of the poor person, a sin that defaces the image of God. From this vantage point and within this reality, the Church must then respond to the de facto sociopolitical world in which it exists. What we have discovered is that this demand is a fundamental one for the faith, and that the Church cannot ignore it." He insists that he is not talking here about a political project; instead, "I am talking of something more profound, something more in keeping with the gospel. I am talking about an authentic option for the poor, of becoming incarnate in their world, of proclaiming the good news to them, of giving them hope, of encouraging them to engage in a liberating praxis, of defending their cause and of sharing their fate."[9]

This, after all, is what Jesus did and what he called his community of followers to do. Jesuit theologian Jon Sobrino, who was a major collaborator in this project of Romero's Church, has reflected that, in bringing the Church to the world of the poor and allowing the Church, the institution, the episcopacy of the Archdiocese of San Salvador, to be truly impacted by that, Romero made the Church a space in which the poor found a home, an authentic expression of their aspirations, a place where their truth could be spoken, where they could become both subject of and collaborator with the pastoral work and the prophetic word of the Church, where this word from and of the poor could open space in which the full force for liberation might run its course. Sobrino wrote:

> What he succeeded in doing was "institutionalizing" the preferential option for the poor. To "institutionalize," in this instance, does not mean to bureaucratize or trivialize. On the contrary, it means that not only should Christians as individuals make this option for the poor but so should the Church as such, placing at the disposal of the poor the resources that the Church, as an institution, has at its own disposal. Precisely because he was the archbishop and therefore the foremost representative of the institutional Church, it became possible to speak of the Church of the poor. Because of him the people could judge the various ecclesiastical institutions by that criterion: the defense of the poor and the oppressed.[10]

This also had implications for how Romero saw the role of institutional power and authority. Romero believed that the Church should be an institution exercising power not from above but from within history and at the service of the people. "The institutional power of the Church," wrote Sobrino, "ought to be exercised through means that are proper to the Church, especially through the word that creates awareness, and not through politico-ecclesiastical means, always on the lookout for concessions from the state. It ought to be exercised for the good of the people, and not for the good of the institution to the detriment of the people."[11]

Church authority as exercised in its decisionmaking was affected as well. While Romero took total responsibility for the decisions he made as archbishop and the teachings expressed in his pastoral letters and homilies, these were also a reflection of broad collaboration with pastoral workers, with base communities, and with the theologians. This collaboration was fundamental to his model of leadership and was still another reason why his words were spoken with such authenticity and relevance. They were a reflection of the national reality and of the witness of the Church within it gleaned from the varied experiences, sufferings, pastoral efforts, and perspectives of the people of God at many levels of society.

What, then, does all of this say about how Archbishop Romero showed a commitment to the institution while at the same time expressing his prophetic and pastoral ministry? Key to answering that question is appreciation of how much Oscar Romero loved his Church. Because of that love, it was essential for him that this Church witness with complete integrity before the people and complete credibility in the word it preached.

Let me share an example of what I mean. Romero was often accused by his opponents within the Salvadoran church hierarchy of creating division, and therefore scandal, within the Church. These complaints, sent to Rome on an ongoing basis, hurt Romero deeply. He understood what it meant to present a divided Church to his people, and indeed he struggled almost daily with this problem. Not only were his efforts at dialogue with his opponents within the Salvadoran Bishops Conference rebuffed, but he found himself the target of conspiracies to undermine his efforts and a campaign to induce the Vatican to assign a coadjutor who would take real authority away from him.

As painful as this was, Romero did not believe that he was the source of scandal. What hurt him deeply was to see fellow bishops, such as the papal nuncio and Bishop Eduardo Alvarez, the military vicar, wedded to the same elite classes and military leaders who were committing massacres, torture, and disappearances; who were killing his priests; and who were defaming the work of the Church. This was, for him, the real scandal to the Church. In his second pastoral letter, we find him lamenting the fact that there were some within the Church who did not contribute to real unity "either out of ignorance, or in order to defend their own interests." He believed some of them to be "anchored in false traditionalism," unwilling to "hear the voice of Vatican II and of Medellín. They have been scandalized at the Church's new face," he said.

But he believed passionately that real unity within the Church rests not in a superficial unity of authority and structure but in the authenticity with which it takes up its commitment to follow Jesus Christ. For him this was expressed in part by the tremendous solidarity that his Church was receiving from within and from outside El Salvador. He saw this solidarity from so many levels—his own priests, religious, lay pastoral leaders, grassroots communities, episcopal conferences in other countries, a growing international faith-based solidarity movement—as a sign of the real unity within the Church and also as a sign of the unifying power of the Church in its true mission.

He wrote, "But, yet again, the events of recent months remind us that Christian unity comes not only from verbal confession of the same faith but also from putting that faith into practice. It arises out of a common effort, a shared mission. It comes from fidelity to the word and to the demands of Jesus Christ, and it is cemented in common suffering. Unity in the Church is not achieved by ignoring the reality of the world in which we live."[12]

This represents a fierce dedication to the institution of the Church. Romero saw his role in part as cleansing the Church of its historical participation in the structural sin that had—and still does—oppress the people of El Salvador. This participation had separated the Church from the very people who are the subjects of its mission, subjects of the gospel of Jesus Christ.

In the same way, Romero was often criticized for presenting an "exclusive" word, of leaving out of his word the rich, the business classes, the elite families of El Salvador, many of whom saw themselves as patrons of the Church. Not so, said Romero. He invited them to participate in the saving action of God by being converted—like Zaccheus. The word he offered them was also one of liberation from structures that oppress others, by liberating themselves from those structures. He longed for this conversion, longed to be able to announce as Jesus did on that evening with Zaccheus, "today salvation has come to this house" (Luke 19:9).

For here, too, there was the scandal of division—division between extremes of rich and poor, between wealthy landowners and the impoverished peasants whose labor they exploited, between factory owners and the workers from whom they withheld a just wage. And in this traditionally Catholic nation the scandal was only deepened by the fact that both sides of the divide often claimed the same Catholic faith. This was the real and scandalous division, and Romero therefore invited all his people to participate in a liberating project that could heal these wounds among God's people. It was not a superficial institutional unity that was his focus, but rather the unity of an institution bound by a common purpose: the individual, social, political, and economic liberation of the whole person, as articulated at the Second Vatican Council and at Medellín. Romero's commitment to the institution of the Church meant being committed, even to the point of martyrdom, to putting that Church at the service of this project. The depth with which Romero felt this commitment is reflected in the joy and gratification that he experienced after his visits to Rome.

For example, Pope Paul VI, for whom Romero held a deep respect and even reverence, encouraged him to remain strong and to be courageous. What this support meant to Romero is clearly expressed in the reflections he wrote in his diary regarding these papal visits. For example, he writes of his 1978 audience with Pope Paul: "The Pope made us sit one on each side of him and addressing himself to me in particular, he took my right hand and kept it between his two hands for a long time. I also took the Pope's hands in my two hands." It was a moment that "expressed such intimate communion between a bishop and the center of Catholic unity."

The pope told him, "I understand your difficult work. It is a work that can be misunderstood; it requires a great deal of patience and a great deal of strength. I already know that not everyone thinks like you do, that it is difficult in the circumstances of your country to have this unanimity of thinking. Nevertheless, proceed with courage, with patience, with strength, with hope."[13] Which is exactly what he did. Friends and colleagues said he came back revitalized by this message of support from "the center of Catholic unity."

Romero never intended to take his Church on any course that would estrange his archdiocese from the universal Church committed to the gospel of Jesus Christ. Instead, what he tried so hard to do, out of his own deep love for the Church, was to make it more and more reflective of the gospel, a carrier of the story of Jesus, a living body recognizable by the people. He sought to make it into a space where people could recognize their truth—and say yes to it. Some might hate him for it and want him dead; others would find themselves born to a new life.

When Romero was first appointed to the episcopate, he chose as his episcopal motto the phrase *sentir con la iglesia*—to be of one mind and heart with the Church. As he lived out his ministry as archbishop of San Salvador, we see that this was not a passive following of the institutional Church's authority, but instead a commitment to build the Church into the body of Christ, into a space ever more identified with Christ, into a Church that promotes, as quoted above, "the solutions that seem most likely to bring the 'reign of God' into being."

[See "Archbishop with an Attitude: Oscar Romero's Sentir con la Iglesia" in the May 2003 issue of *Studies in the Spirituality of Jesuits* for an excellent, in-depth study of how and why Monsignor Romero struggled so fervently to reconcile his loyalty and obedience to the hierarchical Church with his commitment to serve the "least brethren" that God had entrusted to his care—and how he succeeded so brilliantly that Vicar General Ricardo Urioste eulogizes him as ". . . a martyr for the Magisterium as well as for the poor, because Romero would never have been so bold had he not believed the teaching of the Church demanded it of him."—Ed.]

What then does Oscar Romero have to say to us in the United States today? What challenge does he pass on to us regarding our commitment to the institutional Church? Were his word and example only for El Salvador at that particular moment in its history, or is there truly some more universal vision of Church embodied here?

Some have tried to minimize Romero's challenge by saying exactly the former—that his word and pastoral model were only meant for El Salvador and, after all, we live in different circumstances, a different "particularity," a different history. But I would challenge us to look more closely at our world, to see its true condition, and ask ourselves what it would mean for our institutional Church here in the United States to ever more deeply immerse itself in the reality of the world. On a global scale—and, increasingly, in our own nation as well—the circumstances we face are all too similar to those of El Salvador. Disparities in wealth are growing; poverty touches countless millions of our sisters and brothers. Structures of injustice actively and aggressively promoted, that now predominate, are pushing millions into death, poverty, misery, and exploitation. The wealth of the minority rests on the backs of impoverished workers and unemployed whose very exploitation supports our ability to consume. Violence pervades this system, with civil wars, massacres, torture, and other forms of degrading human treatment all too common in our world. We are even at the point where our level of consumption is threatening the environment that sustains our human life on this planet.

In El Salvador we found out that Romero's history was also our history, and that our story was part of the story of El Salvador. Along with this history, we also share the social teachings of the Church, emboldened now in its critique of economic systems that are causing such injustice and misery in our world. So what must the Church look like in this world if it is to authentically be the body of Christ still present in our history? How must it organize itself in order to have its word immediately recognized as authentic truth about the human condition, about sin, and about the saving action of God within this history?

It is the challenge that I articulated in the beginning—a challenge to ask ourselves once again what the Church was created to be and what mission it is to serve. It is a challenge to put the Church at the service of the reign of God in a continuously flowing and evolving manner, to assess the needs and aspirations of the suffering people, whose wretchedness defies the imagination, suffering the permanent mockery of the wealth of our incredible levels of consumption and expectations regarding lifestyle—and to do so from their vantage point.

Finally, I would remind us once again as I conclude these reflections that Romero revitalized his Church. The authenticity of his witness caused vocations to rise, brought the energies of hundreds of catechists and Delegates of the Word into the pastoral work of the Church, revitalized parishes, and gave energy to the base community movement. Thousands upon thousands of Salvadorans were willing to follow the word of the Church, even in the face of persecution, because the gospel had become alive for them.

Thus, from the commitment of Oscar Romero to his Church we have a lesson to learn about how to renew life and energy within the institution. In a speech delivered at Georgetown University upon receiving an honorary doctorate, Romero said, "The Church has the same task as before—that of redeeming persons from sin and leading them to eternal life—but it starts from the situation in this world where there exists the duty of planting the reign of God now."[14]

This implies making the institution fertile ground where the seeds can be planted and nurtured. This is what Romero did, and in doing so he left us a legacy of great love for and fidelity to the institutional life of the Church.

NOTES

1. Archbishop Oscar Romero, *Voice of the Voiceless: The Four Pastoral Letters and Other Statements,* trans. Michael J. Walsh (Maryknoll, N.Y.: Orbis Books, 1985), 70.

2. Ibid., 73.

3. Ibid., 74.

4. Romero, "The Church's Mission amid the National Crisis," in *Voice,* 150.

5. Ibid., 130.

6. "The Political Dimension of the Faith from the Perspective of the Option for the Poor," in *Voice,* 179–80.

7. Ibid., 180.

8. Ibid., 182–83.

9. Ibid., 182.

10. Jon Sobrino, "A Theologian's View of Oscar Romero," in Romero, *Voice,* 31.

11. Ibid., 38.

12. Romero, *Voice,* 81.

13. *Archbishop Oscar Romero: A Shepherd's Diary,* trans. Irene B. Hodgson (Cincinnati: St. Anthony Messenger Press, 1993), 69.

14. Romero, *Voice,* 164.

6

Monsignor Oscar A. Romero

Martyr of the Option for the Poor

(2003)

SAMUEL RUIZ GARCÍA

Although much time has passed since 24 March 1980, the date of the assassination of Monsignor Oscar A. Romero, the presence of Monsignor Romero continues to live and to grow. Monsignor Romero continues to live in his people. His presence is a sociological fact, a cultural and political deed. It is part of the Latin American reality and, what is more surprising, it forms part of the continent's future. One has to take him into account in order to relate Latin America's history.

A group of Latin American bishops signed a document on 29 March 1980 which cited "three things we admire and give thanks for in the episcopacy of Monsignor Oscar A. Romero":

"He was in the first place a proclaimer of the faith and teacher of the truth. . . . Second, he was a zealous defender of justice. . . . Third, he was the friend, the brother, and the defender of the poor and oppressed, of the peasant, of the worker, of those who have been marginalized. Monsignor Romero has been an exemplary bishop because he has been a bishop of the poor in a continent which carries so cruelly the stamp of the poverty of the vast majority. He inserted himself among them, defended their cause, and suffered the same fate as they: persecution and martyrdom.

Monsignor Romero is the symbol of an entire Latin American Church and continent, a true suffering servant of Yahweh who is burdened with the sin of injustice and with the death of our continent.

Although we sometimes dreaded it, his assassination has not surprised us. His destiny could be no other if he was true to Jesus, if he entered truly into the pain of our people. We know, however, that the death of Monsignor Romero is not an isolated incident. It is part of the testimony for which a Church in Medellín and Puebla opted for the Gospel for the poor and oppressed. The martyrdom of Monsignor Romero enables us to better understand permanent realities among our people: death from hunger and illness; innumerable martyrdoms and countless crosses which mark our continent; the thousands of workers, students, priests, sisters, pastoral agents, and bishops who are jailed, tortured, and murdered for their belief in Jesus Christ and for their love of the poor. These martyrdoms, like the death of Jesus, are not only the fruits of the injustice of man but also the seed of resurrection.

Mons. Oscar A. Romero is a martyr of the liberation that the gospel demands, a living example of the pastor which Puebla wanted.

Who Are the Poor Today?

In a real, not a metaphoric, sense the poor are those who fundamentally suffer from need. They are those who are denied the material goods necessary for a dignified existence. They are those who are marked by insecurity. They are those who die ahead of their time. The poor can be described, at least in part, with three statements: they are a collective phenomenon; they are the product of a conflict-ridden process; they plead for an alternative historical plan.

The Poor Are a Collective Phenomenon

Poverty today is not only a massive problem but also a social and structural condition. The poor comprise entire towns as well as entire social classes. They constitute the vast majority of the population in Latin America: i.e., 80 percent, compared to a middle class of 15 percent and an upper-middle or upper class of 5 percent. An empirical or vulgar view, which conceives the poor as isolated individuals or as atypical cases, must be discarded. This outdated but still prevalent conception sees two causes for the phenomenon of poverty: moral defect of the victims (such as ignorance or laziness) and natural causes (being born poor, or the existence of both rich and poor since the time of Adam and Eve).

This distorted view must give way to "assistancism." It is essential to give the poor what they most need: alms, schools, and other vital services. Naturally, those who do so are the saviors of the poor. They are heeding Christ's call to comfort his "least brethren." But these individualized forms of aid are not enough.

The majority of the religious initiatives of the past century, and even today, were animated by the objective of helping the poor with a compassion that was evangelical but not analytical. Such an approach sees the individual suffering but not the collective causes; it sees the persons, but not the structures that surround them. Poverty has not diminished as a result of these well-intentioned initiatives. Rather, it grew.

The Poor Are the Result of a Conflict-Ridden Process

Contrary to simplistic theories, the poor are a manufactured social phenomenon rather than a natural fact. They are systematically impoverished and oppressed by the forces of a system of domination. In the words of the synodal fathers:

> Luxury of the few becomes an insult against the misery of the huge masses. This is contrary to the plan of the Creator and contrary to the honor due to Him. . . . The Church discerns a situation of social sin, of even more gravity because it happens in so-called Catholic countries which have the capacity to change. (Puebla 28)
>
> This poverty is not a natural stage, but rather the product of economic, social, and political situations and structures, although there are other causes of destitution. The internal state of our countries which, in many cases, finds its origin and support in mechanisms which, because they are impregnated not with an authentic humanism but with materialism, produce on an international level rich who are ever more rich at the expense of the poor who are ever more poor. This reality demands, then, personal conversion and profound changes in the structures which respond to the legitimate aspirations of the people for a true social justice;

changes which have not occurred or have been too slow in the experience of Latin America. (Puebla 30)

The situation of generalized extreme poverty acquires in real life concrete faces in which we should recognize the suffering traits of Christ, the Lord, which questions and implores us. (Puebla 31)

The Poor Ask for an Alternative Social Plan

Given that the situation of the poor has a structural root, its liberation happens through the change of social structures that prohibit them from growing and affirming themselves historically. The poor who live in today's society orient the perspectives of change toward a new society, and for that reason the poor are bound to the idea of a change in the basics of the social system. That which was formerly an ideal has become a concrete plan for a society which no longer allows the few to dominate the many, and which no longer suffers privation of vital necessities such as food, housing, clothing, elementary education, and basic health care.

We can see that poverty today does not have the same nature as it had in the past. It no longer consists simply of absence or delay in material development; rather, it is primarily the fruit of contradictory development which enables the rich to grow richer while the poor grow poorer. In social terms, today's poverty signifies oppression and dependence; ethically, it signifies injustice and social sin. We affirm that the poor exist because of structures of exploitation and exclusion.

There are major flaws in the functionalist view which reads poverty as a collective (but not conflictive) reality, in which the poor are merely held back, kept in an underdeveloped state, and denied the fruits of progress. This view implies that the poor can join the "developed" classes merely by waiting for assistance from the rich and privileged. But this was the theory and methodology of the "Alliance for Progress" which failed during the 1960s, initiating awareness that the real need was not for "development" but rather for liberation.

Option for the Poor in the Old Testament

It would seem unnecessary to emphasize that God speaks in the Bible. In the common understanding of our western culture God is the only perfect being, omnipotent and omniscient, the creator of heaven and earth, whose goodness and justice cannot be surpassed. But we have learned in Latin America, through the conflicts that occurred between Christians, that a common belief in an only God hides different and sometimes opposed ways of conceiving of this creator God. Nevertheless, we can say that the God who speaks in the Bible is the God who led Israel out of Egypt (in the Old Testament) and the God who raised Jesus Christ from the dead (in the New Testament). This is, therefore, the God who created heaven and earth, and the perfection of love of God demands that he be universal. Yet, this concrete expression of universal love preferred the slaves in Egypt and the poor of Galilee in Palestine. God's love for the pharaoh was surpassed by his preferential love of the slaves; likewise his love for the Pharisees and scribes was surpassed by the love and solidarity God felt for the sinners and the women of Galilee. Thus, the God of the Bible who is the creator of heaven and earth takes on a specific profile: "I am Yahweh, your God who brought you out of the land of Egypt, out of the house of slavery. You shall have no other gods beside me" (Exod. 20:2–3).

These phrases are so familiar to us that it might seem that we need not reflect further on them. Nevertheless, it happens that they are not so obvious. Above all, Yahweh presents himself in a polemical tone against the other possible gods. The text does not deny the existence of other gods, nor does it affirm it. Their existence or nonexistence is irrelevant. What *is* relevant is that you, Israelite and designee of this law, begin your justice with the prohibition to render cult and allegiance to other gods. In other words, any god who has not brought you out of Egypt cannot be your God.

"I am Yahweh, your God" contains message within message. The proper name Yahweh serves to assure us that those gods who could not or would not deliver the faithful from slavery in Egypt cannot hide behind a generic title of "God." The great narrative traditions of the Pentateuch concur in placing the revelation of this divine name in the context of the Exodus.

Bringing Israel out of servitude in the land of Egypt is why Yahweh is the God of Israel. This liberation establishes a relationship of exclusive dependence on Yahweh. It is impossible to adore Yahweh without confessing oneself a freed slave. According to Exodus 18:38 a heterogeneous multitude left Egypt; their unity had to be created by the exodus.

The rubrics for Passover reveal how the nation continued defining itself. The uncircumcised are prohibited from eating the Passover meal. Foreigners who wish to celebrate the Passover of Yahweh must circumcise all the males of the family before participating as a part of the nation (Exod. 12:43, 48).

In other words, you must unite yourself to those who celebrate liberation from slavery in order for Yahweh to be your God. None who are in solidarity with the liberated people, marking themselves through circumcision, shall be excluded from the community that celebrates its liberation from Egypt. In practice, this was not so simple for Israel, but we are expressing an intention: Yahweh is your God. The God of Exodus is a God who hears the cries of the slaves, who freed them and took them to a land flowing with milk and honey. The principal credential of Moses, chosen by Yahweh to lead the exodus, was that he risked his high social position when he killed an Egyptian who abused a Hebrew slave (Exod. 2:11–15).

The story of the exodus makes it clear that justice demands that one take a position at the side of the oppressed, just as Yahweh does. The impartiality of God does not preclude his preferential love for the orphan and the widow. Similarly, in a situation of oppression, he makes a preferential option for the poor. Yahweh's options for the oppressed, being an integral element of the exodus that has founding character for Israel, exerts a basic influence on almost all the materials of the Bible.

Option for the Poor in the New Testament

If the people of God appear in the New Testament as the "chosen" and as the heirs of the promises, it is because they are a people poor and oppressed. The logic of the Incarnation should be understood not only as a divine "condescension," in which the Son of God assumes our humanity (while concealing his divinity) to make himself the Son of man. Rather, he takes on a voluntary poverty having been born in Bethlehem of Judah, where Mary, his mother, by Quirinus's decree, set out together with Joseph, who represented in the home the Heavenly Father.

The angel of the Lord appeared to the shepherds who lived in the countryside surrounding Bethlehem, surrounding them with his brightness and proclaiming, "Do not fear because I come to announce to you good news which shall be the cause of great joy for all the people. Today was born for you in the city of David a savior who is Christ the Lord" (Luke 2:10–11). After living the experience of the desert in Egypt and then returning to the simplicity of Nazareth, where he lived as the son of a carpenter, Jesus grew in wisdom, age, and grace before God and before humanity, waiting for a sign to begin his public life. This sign appeared with the imprisonment and death of the Precursor, John the Baptist.

After traveling through the communities and seeing the multitudes as sheep without a shepherd, Jesus entered the synagogue of Nazareth. From the book of the prophet Isaiah, he read aloud: "The Spirit of the Lord is upon me, for He has anointed me to bring Good News to the poor, to announce liberty to captives, and that the blind shall soon see; to set free the oppressed and to proclaim a year of good favor from the Lord." He returned the scroll and announced, "Today these prophecies that you have just heard are accomplished" (Luke 4:17–21). Jesus' option for the poor provoked indignation and rejection by his audience. They dragged him from the city to the top of a hill, intending to hurl him off the cliff. But he passed through the midst of them and went on his way (Luke 4:28–30).

A great logical and vital congruence are, then, the Beatitudes, the Magna Carta of the Kingdom. Jesus awakens hope among the multitudes and invites them to rise from their prostration, but he also obliges them to expand their view. The kingdom that the poor will receive will not make them rich and comfortable; happiness is promised in the midst of persecutions.

There is no discontinuity between the Old and New Testament, since Christ did not come to abolish the Law but rather to perfect it and give it fullness.

While speaking of the greatest commandments of the old law, Jesus puts the second commandment—to love one's neighbor as one's self—on the same plane as the first commandment—to love God over all things (Matt. 22:37–40), and he combines love of God and love for one's neighbor into a single new commandment (John 13:34). As John the apostle clearly understood, Jesus was saying that one cannot love God without loving him in one's neighbor (John 2:7–10 and 4:20–21). Furthermore, the degree to which we have or have not loved our neighbor during times of misfortune reflects our love of God himself, and this is a question we will all have to answer in the final judgment (Matt. 25:32–46).

Option for the Poor in the Church: Second Vatican Council

Among the objectives of the Second Vatican Council were two fundamental questions posed by Pope John XXIII: how to speak of God to those who do not believe in God; how Christians, often so divided against themselves, could become witnesses for the non-Christians. On 2 October 1962, shortly before the opening of the Council, the Holy Father added, "There is a third enlightening point—the Church, in the presence of peoples on the way to development, discovers what it is and what it should be: the Church of the poor, that is the Church of everyone."

This synthetic expression contains a great density of thought: that the option for the poor is not truly optional, but rather constitutive of the Church; that it is a procedural option which requires timely review; that it does not relate solely to the individual poor but rather to those who are products of the social structure (i.e., "peoples on the way to development"); that being Church of the poor produces a universal Church, since only an imposed Church could come from higher socioeconomic levels; that this Church of the poor calls out to all and is, therefore, inclusive; that the necessity of conversion exists for the poor as well as the wealthy because all of humankind should work to construct the kingdom of God as a just society, including those who are direct causes of marginalization.

Although the first two points were adequately treated in the Council, the third could not be treated with the profundity required. Despite some poverty, Europe was solidly rooted in the first world, while pervasive, crushing, and institutionalized poverty was concentrated primarily in the Southern Hemisphere. The primarily European leadership of the Council lacked the experiential and pastoral background necessary for theological reflection upon what was, for them, a strange and little-understood phenomenon.

In practice, the Church of peoples on the way to development was not ignored by the documents of the Council, but the Council fathers knew that more profound consideration was needed.

Option for the Poor in the Church: Medellín, Puebla, and Santo Domingo

When the bishops of Latin America gathered in Medellín, Puebla, and Santo Domingo, they recognized that the Holy Father's first two mandates (speaking about God to atheists and agnostics, and giving witness to non-Christians) were primarily first-world realities since, at that time, there were very few non-Christians in Latin America. Conversely, the third point was an almost universal reality throughout the nations of Latin America.

It was vital, they realized, that the Gospel be announced to the "non-humans," to those being crushed by socioeconomic and political systems.

They pronounced the "option for the poor," perceiving that there is no juxta-position of the world of poverty and the world of wealth, but rather a causal relationship between the two—that there are rich because there are poor, and vice versa. Hence, the announcement of the Gospel and the action of build-ing the kingdom of God are conceived as "liberation" from the situation of sin within the current system.

"The Latin American Episcopacy," said the bishops in Medellín, "cannot remain indifferent before the enormous social injustices existing in Latin America, injustices that maintain the majority of our people, in very many cases, on the verge of inhuman misery."

"A silent clamor gushes from millions of people, asking their pastors for a liberation which does not come from anywhere. 'You are now listening to us in silence, but we hear the cry which arises from your suffering,' said the Pope to the peasants in Colombia" (Medellín, Doc.14, *Poverty of the Church* nn. 1 and 2).

Similarly, the bishops wrote: "If 'development is the new name of peace' (Pope Paul VI, Populorum Progressio), the Latin American underdevelop-ment, with particular characteristics of the different countries, is an unjust situation promoting tensions that conspire against peace. . . . In speaking of a situation of injustice, we refer to these realities that express a situation of sin" (Medellín, Doc. 2, *Peace*).

"Christ, our Savior, not only loved the poor but rather 'being rich he became poor'; he lived in poverty; he centered his mission on the announce-ment to the poor of their liberty and he founded his Church as a sign of that poverty among people. . . . The present situation demands, therefore, of bish-ops, priests, religious, and the laity, the spirit of poverty which 'breaking the bonds of selfish possession of material goods, stimulates the Christian to organically dispose the economy and power toward the benefit of the commu-nity' (Pope Paul VI, "Address at the Mass for the Day of Development," Bogotá, 23 August 1968). The poverty of the Church and of her members in Latin America should be sign and commitment—sign of the immeasurable value of the poor in the eyes of God, and commitment to solidarity with those who suffer" (Medellín, Doc. 14, *Poverty of the Church*, n. 7).

Subsequent reflection in the meetings of CELAM at Puebla and Santo Domingo refer to the indigenous people as the poorest of the poor. The option for them is required by Christ himself and ". . . by the scandalous reality of the economic imbalances in Latin America that should lead to the establishment of a human co-existence which is dignified and fraternal, and the construction of a just and free society" (Medellín pt. 4, ch. 1), and by the call ". . . to live and announce the demands of Christian poverty; the Church should review her structures and the life of her members, above all of the agents of the ministry, with a view toward an effective conversion" (Medellín, 1157).

"This conversion carries with it the requirement of an austere lifestyle and a total trust in the Lord since, in the evangelical activity of the Church, she can count more on the being and power of God and of his grace than with 'having more' and with secular power. Thus, she will present an image authentically poor, open to God and to neighbor, always available, where the poor have the real capacity for participation and are recognized for their worth" (Medellín, 1158).

The Option of Monsignor Oscar A. Romero: The Situation at the Time of His Installation

When Monsignor Oscar A. Romero was named archbishop of the Archdiocese of San Salvador on 8 February 1977, El Salvador was already living in a state of repression and persecution of the most committed sectors of the Salvadoran Church.

On 3 February, the government exiled a former Spanish Jesuit to Guatemala after torturing him for ten days. On the eve of Monsignor Romero's installation, Fr. Rafael Barahona was kidnapped and brutally beaten by the authorities. Fr. Rutilio Grande was murdered on 12 March, along with Mr. Manuel Soloranzo and the youth Nelson Rutilio Lemus. That same day, Fr. Barahona's brother was murdered in San Juan Tepezontes.

Stance in Regard to the Murder of Fr. Rutilio Grande

Monsignor Romero immediately asked President Molina for a full investigation of the events. When the government failed to do its duty, Monsignor Romero excommunicated those responsible for the assassination; he formed a standing committee to monitor human rights; he ordered the closing of Catholic schools and colleges for three days; and he cancelled all of the nation's religious services on Sunday, 20 March, except for a Mass over which he personally presided in the Cathedral of San Salvador. After announcing that he would not participate in any governmental ceremonies until government resolved the situation, Monsignor Romero declined to attend the installation of the new president several months later.

His Homilies

In the funeral Mass of Fr. Rutilio Grande, Monsignor Romero affirmed, "If this were a simple funeral, I would speak here of human and personal relationships with Fr. Rutilio Grande, whom I regard as a brother. In culminating moments of my life he was very close to me and those gestures are never forgotten. But it is not time for personal thoughts, but rather [a time] to pick up from this corpse a message for all of us who continue on the pilgrimage. Pope Paul VI says, 'The Church offers to this liberating struggle of the world liberating people, but to those she gives an inspiration of faith, a social doctrine, which is at the base of her prudence and of her existence to be translated into concrete commitments, and over all a motivation of love, of fraternal love.' True love is what brings Rutilio to his death taking two farmers by the hand. In this way he loves the Church, he dies with them, and with them he presents himself for the transcendence to heaven. He loves them, and it is significant that while Fr. Grande walked forward for his people to take the message of the Mass and of salvation, this is where he fell pierced with many holes. The love of the Lord inspires the action of Rutilio Grande. Dear priests, let us take up this precious inheritance."

In the funeral of Fr. Alfonso Navarro Oviedo, 12 May 1977, Monsignor Oscar Arnulfo Romero displayed what has been called a process of conversion: "Here we promise, before the corpse of a dead priest, what we said in the communiqué of a few days ago: we wish to ratify our vow of fidelity to the Word of God, of fidelity to the Magisterium of the Church. And with this motivation . . . we will feel the courage of the first apostles to say, 'it is not legal to obey humans before obeying God.' This is the flag which cannot fall. If we are going to entomb a brother of ours, we do not beat ourselves in defeat; we feel that we are missing a soldier in our ranks, but we feel that someone has to fill the remaining space."

Capacity to Recognize His Faults and Ask for Forgiveness

A disposition toward admitting his mistakes was an attractive aspect of the personality of Monsignor Romero. This was evidenced in two visits which he made to the Christian community of Zacamil, a poor neighborhood on the outskirts of the city. The first visit in 1972, when he was auxiliary of San Salvador, was to celebrate the Eucharist but also to discuss a pronouncement of the Bishops' Conference regarding the military's attack upon the National University. Eighty people were killed; many were beaten; there was great destruction of property. While many in the community condemned the violence and the injustice, Monsignor Romero defended the military's actions because of ostensible communist infiltration among the students. The monsignor said, "The work you do here is political, not pastoral. You have not invited me here to celebrate the Eucharist but to a subversive meeting." Father Pedro DeClercq, who had invited Monsignor Romero, removed his alb and stole and put them on the altar, saying, "We cannot celebrate the Eucharist in these conditions. There will be no Mass." Monsignor Romero left alone. Six years later, Romero returned to Zacamil to be welcomed as the new archbishop. He immediately mentioned his earlier visit: "You remember that we couldn't even celebrate the Eucharist. I remember very well; today, as your pastor, I want to tell you that I now understand what happened, and publicly before you I admit that I made a mistake. I was wrong. You were right. That day you gave me a lesson on faith, a lesson on what the Church is. Please forgive me for what happened."

Relying on others to obtain advice does not diminish the coherence or the force of his message. He was well aware that "a preaching that is not incarnated in reality can have pretty, pious considerations that do not bother anyone," but that a true preaching of Christ should awaken, illuminate, and disturb the sinner. "Naturally, a preaching has to encounter conflict, has to lose misunderstood prestige, has to bother, has to be persecuted. It cannot sit well with the powers of darkness and sin."

Monsignor Romero, who attended the Third General Conference of Latin American Bishops in Puebla in 1979, identified completely with the call of the bishops to "the conversion of the entire Church to the preferential option for the poor, with intentions of her integral liberation." That is how, in a country torn apart by violence, Monsignor Romero read with complete clarity "the subversive testimony of the Beatitudes, which have turned everything on end." He understood that violence had to be removed from its foundations in social injustice and structural violence, and he recognized that it is the duty of the Church "to recognize the mechanisms which engender poverty." He knew that the preferential option for the poor is an invitation for the Church as a whole, but also for each follower of Christ. "The Christian that does not wish to live this commitment of solidarity with the poor is not worthy to be called

Christian," he said, adding, "The poor have therefore marked out the true path of the Church. A Church that does not bind itself with the poor to denounce from among the poor the injustices that are committed is not the true Church of Jesus Christ" (Homily, 23 September 1979)

Similarly, he recognized his own charge as an archbishop: "This denunciation . . . I believe to be an obligation in my position as shepherd of the people who suffer injustice. The Gospel imposes it on me, for which I am ready to confront trial and imprisonment" (Homily, 14 May 1978).

With much clarity, in his homily of 8 July 1979, he said: "If they were to cut off our radio station, if they were to suppress the newspaper, and if a population would have no priests, each one of you should become a microphone of God; each one of you should be a messenger and a prophet."

During a four-day retreat with a group of priests of the Vicariate of Chalatenango, Monsignor Romero wrote: "Another fear of mine is with regard to the risks to my life. It is difficult to accept a violent death that in these circumstances is most possible. . . . Father Azcue [Romero's confessor] has encouraged me, telling me that my disposition should be to give my life for God whatever should be my end. I should live unknown circumstances with the grace of God. He has assisted the martyrs and, if it would be necessary, I will feel Him near me when I take my last breath. But what is more important than the moment of death is to give Him my whole life, to live for Him."

Two weeks before his death, in an interview with the Mexican magazine *Excelsior,* he said: "I have been frequently threatened with death. I should tell you that, as a Christian, I do not believe in death without Resurrection. If they kill me, I will rise again in the Salvadoran people. I tell you without any boasting, with the greatest humility. . . . As a pastor, I am obliged by Divine order to give my life for those whom I love, who are all Salvadorans, even for those who will murder me. If they succeed in their threats, from now I already obey God. I offer my blood for the redemption and resurrection of El Salvador. . . . Martyrdom is a grace of God that I do not believe I deserve. But if God accepts the sacrifice of my life, may my blood be seed of liberation and sign that hope would soon be a reality. My death, if it is accepted by God, will be for the liberation of my people and a testimony of hope in the future. You could say if they should kill me that I forgive and bless those who do it."

There is no doubt that the death of Monsignor Romero had a martyr-like character. We see that in Latin America an era is beginning in which Christians, dying for the faith, give their lives for justice.

7

Rutilio and Romero

Martyrs for Our Time

(1997)

DEAN BRACKLEY, S.J.

Although we might honor the memory of Archbishop Romero in many different ways, I propose to reflect with you on both Oscar Romero and Rutilio
Grande, the Jesuit priest who was El Salvador's proto-martyr. Rutilio heads the
list of eighteen priests, one archbishop, five religious sisters, and hundreds of
catechists who were slain in El Salvador between 1977 and 1992 for the faith, for
the poor, and for speaking the truth. They mixed their blood with seventy-five
thousand others in that country who dared to dream of a future that would
be different.

Bishop Pedro Casadáliga of Brazil warns us, "Woe to that people that for-
gets its martyrs!" But in times of junk media and bad news, we can easily forget the good news of even the recent martyrs. In his apostolic letter on the
preparation for the third millennium, Pope John Paul has called for recovering
the testimony of the martyrs of this century. "At the end of the second millennium, the church has once again become a church of martyrs," he writes. "The
recent martyrdoms in Algeria and Central Africa have again brought this
home to us. This witness must not be forgotten. The church of the first centuries took care to write down in special martyrologies the witness of the
martyrs. . . . In our own century the martyrs have returned, many of them
nameless, 'unknown soldiers' as it were of God's great cause . . . the local

churches should do everything possible to ensure that the memory of those who have suffered martyrdom should be safeguarded, gathering the necessary documentation."

It is especially appropriate to recover the memory of Rutilio and Romero, who represent the best of that "church of the poor" which promises so much for the universal church and for the world. I will focus on Rutilio's life and ministry, of which we know less, and on his relationship to Romero. Secondly, I will offer a few reflections on what Rutilio and Romero, and the Central American martyrs generally, say to us today.

Lives Found, Lives Encountered

A few years ago a co-worker of Rutilio wrote a book with the poetic title *Romero-Rutilio vidas encontradas.* In Spanish, *vidas encontradas* means "lives found." Rutilio and Romero lost their lives, and so "found" them as the Gospel says. But the expression also means lives that met. Their two lives encountered one another—with momentous consequences. Many have drawn parallels between the relationship of Rutilio to Romero and that of John the Baptist to Jesus himself.

Oscar Arnulfo Romero was born in 1917 in the poor eastern town of Ciudad Barrios where he grew up. After minor seminary and one year of major seminary, he was sent to study theology in Rome, where he was ordained in 1942. After another year of studies, he returned to his native diocese of San Miguel, where he worked for twenty-three years in parishes and as secretary of the diocese. Padre Romero was renowned for his pastoral zeal, including his excellent preaching and his concern for the poor. But he had no appreciation of the dynamic relationship between wealth and misery, much less a grasp of its implications for the faith.

In 1967, he was sent to San Salvador as secretary of the National Bishops' Conference. Ordained a bishop himself in 1970, he was named head of the southeastern diocese of Santiago de Maria in 1974. It was here, in the face of the growing abuse of the rural poor, that Romero began to grasp the structural causes of poverty and the nature of state-sponsored repression. In early 1977, at the height of national crisis and at the behest of conservative sectors of society, Romero was named archbishop of San Salvador. As we know, Romero rose to the occasion, championing the persecuted poor in the name of Christ for three dramatic years until an assassin silenced his prophetic voice 24 March 1980. He was sixty-two.

Romero's friend Rutilio Grande was gunned down on the way to celebrate Mass in El Paisnal just three weeks after the installation of Romero as archbishop. Rutilio had been born in El Paisnal, a very poor rural town about thirty-three miles north of San Salvador, almost forty-nine years before. His parents separated when he was three or four years old, and he was raised by his pious grandmother and an older brother. Neighbors recall him as a timid and pious child; no one was surprised when he entered the diocesan minor seminary at the age of thirteen. The new archbishop, Luis Chávez y Gonzalez, had recruited the boy while on a pastoral visit to El Paisnal, and the two would remain friends for life. The Jesuits ran the diocesan seminary, and in 1945 Rutilio entered the Society of Jesus. He spent most of his long years of formation in South America and Europe and was ordained in Spain in 1959. After returning to El Salvador he was sent in 1963 to Belgium to study at Lumen Vitae for two years.

Between 1950 and 1971, first as a seminarian and later as a priest, Rutilio worked as teacher and prefect of students in the diocesan seminary in San Salvador, still run by the Jesuits during those years. In 1972 Archbishop Chávez and the Jesuit provincial named him pastor of Aguilares, five miles from El Paisnal. Many had high hopes for what the Aguilares experiment might contribute to pastoral renewal in the archdiocese as a whole. As we shall see, they would not be disappointed. Aguilares demonstrated Rutilio's extraordinary pastoral ability, his uncanny gift for communicating with the poor, his great zeal, and his generosity. He had enjoyed success in his seminary work, in the Jesuit high school, and in pastoral work, winning the trust and respect of those who knew him. This is all the more remarkable since Rutilio suffered from chronic emotional disturbance. In 1950 he had suffered a severe breakdown, was hospitalized with catatonic schizophrenia, and was given only a 60 percent chance of recovery. Afterward, Jesuit superiors doubted his aptness for the order and expected him to leave it. Rutilio recovered, but he would continue to suffer greatly from milder crises that sapped his energy. He remained forever somewhat melancholic and withdrawn, highly sensitive, irritable, at times paralyzed by indecision. But with time he learned to manage his inner turmoil, carrying his cross within. Here we have one of many imperfect parallels between Rutilio and Romero. For his part, Romero's enemies also tried to discredit him as mentally ill. The accusation had no basis in fact. But he did have tendencies to obsessive perfectionism, authoritarian rigidity, and timidity. Before becoming archbishop, insecurity and awkwardness among other tendencies led him to withdraw into his work. But he, too, overcame these limitations, especially as archbishop. For all of us neurotics, Romero and Rutilio, especially, are a genuine inspiration!

The two had come to know each other in 1967, ten years before Rutilio's death, when Romero came to San Salvador as secretary to the Bishops' Conference. Romero lived in the seminary where Rutilio also lived and worked. Both men were shy, and Romero interacted little with the seminarians or the Jesuits. In those years he opposed those who, like Rutilio, were calling for pastoral renewal and social change.

Nevertheless, when Romero was ordained bishop in 1970, he accepted Rutilio's offer to plan and direct the ceremony, for Rutilio was an accomplished liturgist with a fine eye for detail. At Rutilio's funeral seven years later, the new archbishop would recall what he considered his friend's unforgettable gestures of kindness at important moments of Romero's life.

The day after Romero's episcopal ordination the "First National Pastoral Week" began, sponsored by the Bishops' Conference, and it revealed a deep crisis in the Salvadoran church. Just a few weeks before, the Central American bishops had assembled and called for implementing the Medellín Conference in Central America. They spoke of the salvation of the whole person, not just "souls." They emphasized the church's mission to the poor, denounced the structural causes of poverty, condemned the violation of basic rights, and called for authentic liberation.

The Pastoral Week in El Salvador was dominated by progressive young priests, religious, and seminarians. Rutilio played a conspicuous role. Conservatives and most bishops stayed home. Assuming the liberation perspective of the Central American bishops' meeting, the *Conclusions of the Pastoral Week* condemned injustice in El Salvador, denounced the church's past complicity in it, and called for a commitment to the cause of the poor. A month later, the Bishops' Conference rejected some of these conclusions as heterodox and named a commission, headed by Bishop Romero, to revise them. Rutilio wrote to the bishops through their secretary, Bishop Romero, trying to head off the intervention, but it was no use. The commission suppressed references to class division, domination, and the call to commitment to the cause of the poor. If that were not enough, the Sacred Congregation of the Clergy chimed in, all the way from Rome, objecting to expressions like "integral salvation" and, in general, the linking of salvation and social liberation. The Vatican also scotched additional references to injustice, to the church's role in forming community leaders among the poor, and to criticism of "magical ritualism."

The whole matter profoundly affected Tilo, as his friends called him. With characteristic respect, he expressed his disagreement first in private and later to a meeting of diocesan clergy. "Personally, I humbly dare to disagree," he declared. "We should have awakened to this painful reality long ago. We waited too long!" For Rutilio, the Bishops' Conference had neglected basic principles of Vatican II and Medellín. Christians in El Salvador had to follow Christ, who defended the poor. He was not a professional politician, but his message judged social institutions. At this very time, 1970, the Jesuits were proposing Rutilio as the next rector of the seminary. He enjoyed the respect of the diocesan clergy and the bishops and had emerged as a gifted leader. The bishops acceded to his preaching the homily in the Cathedral of San Salvador on the Feast of the Transfiguration, which is the feast of the Savior, the national patron. It was just a few weeks after the Pastoral Week. Rutilio's homily, in the presence of the bishops and top government officials, reflected his growing understanding of the social implications of the Gospel. He spoke of the "Christian revolution based on the essence of the Gospel, whose nucleus is love, and which excludes no one. . . . Christ is our Liberator. He is Liberator of every person and the whole person, body and soul. This transfiguration has to reach out to the public arena to work, to business, to politics, to the encounter with all human beings."

Rutilio asked, "Is the average Salvadoran transfigured? Are the immense majority of our Salvadoran people—the farm workers—transfigured? Is the other minority—the one that has in its hands the economic means, the power of decision, the control of the press and of all the communications media? We have to make painful confessions. . . . Many baptized persons . . . are not transfigured in their mind and in their heart and put up a dike of egoism against the Message of Jesus the Savior."

Rutilio then cited some of the most powerful passages of Paul VI's *Populorum Progressio*, recalling that the president of the country, who was present in the congregation, had promised to let the encyclical guide him during his presidential mandate. Rutilio assured the president that the Church would support him in pursuing the "total, integral and true transfiguration" which the pope had called for and which was necessary if Salvadorans were to enjoy the freedom which the national flag proclaimed should be theirs. Soon after this homily, the bishops, except for the archbishop and his auxiliary, rejected Rutilio as rector of the seminary. He hardly coveted the post, but the bishops' rejection sent him into a dizzying, emotional crisis. Leaving the seminary, he spent a dismal 1971 working at the Jesuit high school in San Salvador. He then traveled to Ecuador, where he spent March to July of 1972 at the Latin American Pastoral Institute (IPLA) and as understudy of Bishop Leonides Proaño in his innovative pastoral work among native peoples in Riobamba. Here Rutilio consolidated the pastoral-theological strategy which he would soon put into practice in Aguilares.

In Ecuador, Tilo's crisis was issuing in a kind of conversion. He now understood that his formation and past work had removed him from his *campesino* roots, and he resolved that, on his return, he would serve the poor directly. Back in El Salvador, the archbishop and the Jesuit provincial were eager to indulge his wishes. From Ecuador, Rutilio wrote to mend relations with the bishops, including Romero, who regretted "incidents that separate persons committed to serve Christ and his Church." The archbishop and the provincial sent Rutilio and an initial collaborator to Aguilares in September of 1972. The parish boundaries embraced thirty-thousand mostly impoverished people, dependent for their livelihood on the surrounding sugar-cane plantations. There were about ten thousand in Aguilares itself and twenty-thousand in surrounding hamlets, including two thousand in El Paisnal. Rutilio recognized that limiting pastoral action to sacraments, traditional cultic practices, and individual morality served to legitimize and preserve the status quo. So, from the beginning, the team pursued a pastoral strategy of evangelization leading to the formation of small communities ("Christian base communities") of genuinely converted "new human beings" capable of understanding and evaluating their situation of extreme poverty in the light of the Gospel and understanding a serious commitment to social change. The pastoral team preached a God who rejects social relations of exploited and exploiters and emphasized that Jesus proclaimed instead God's plan for a new world of brother and sister relationships.

Rutilio and three other Jesuit priests spent the first eight months in Aguilares running parish missions, first in ten sectors of Aguilares and then in each of twenty-seven hamlets. Each mission lasted two weeks and consisted mostly of small-group reflection on gospel passages. It ended with the commissioning of Delegates of the Word who would serve the new base communities. The missions achieved an enormous impact among the *campesinos*. A new consensus began to take hold in the parish. The God who liberates began to displace the God who punishes. "Salvation" came to be understood as the "Reign of God," which begins here on earth. God's will came to mean not obeying abstract moral laws, but following Jesus. Rutilio tirelessly repeated: "God is not in the clouds, lying in a hammock; God acts, and He wants you to construct the Reign of God here on earth." Magical liturgical rites were transformed into celebrations that unified, stirred hope, and stimulated believers to action.

As one parishioner testified: "For me Jesus Christ is our guide. . . . He wanted to transform the world. . . . He was on the side of the poor, he demanded that justice and love and understanding and peace be done. He told us to love each other as he had loved us. . . . He threw down the mighty from their thrones."

Another testified: "The majority of the people now give the name sin to social sin, like dominating each other, taking advantage of each other. Before, they didn't think that way, but now they do."

In the Corpus Christi procession of 1974, base communities carried banners reflecting the new understanding of the faith. One read, "In the name of the Body of Christ, we ask that no more garbage be dumped in the Florida neighborhood, Mr. Mayor." Another banner announced, "We protest against the rich who have appropriated the lands that God gave to all of us and not to just a few. We cannot remain silent about this."

The evangelization spread like brushfire through the region. In 1976, just four and a half years later, a survey revealed that thirteen out of twenty-two rural communities were meeting five times a week. About seven-hundred people met regularly, and 219 adults had experienced more advanced courses in formation in the parish. As the Corpus Christi banners suggested, the fruits of the evangelization had quickly spilled over into the public arena. Without seeking it, the newly conscientized parishioners and the Jesuits entered into the first of many conflicts with landowners, public officials, and administrators of the sugar-cane refineries. In the first encounter on 24 May 1973 at the La Cabana refinery, workers challenged abusive administrators and for the first time they won. Delegates of the Word were among the leaders. Actions like this provoked work speedups, firings, evictions, and charges of "communism."

Rutilio insisted that the pastoral team had no political plan and was tied to no party or political organization. The team not only feared that accusations of partisan politics would undermine the pastoral effort; they also feared that political parties would manipulate the Christian communities and the parish during election campaigns. But the challenge was also closer to home.

What was the proper role for the parish vis-à-vis the unjust social order? From the beginning, some more radical priests had wanted the pastoral team to give priority to political work and organization. There was no *campesino* organization in the region at the time, and the parish was ripe for harvest. The entire nation was polarizing, and organization of the poor would soon spread through the country. The team recognized the need to organize the *campesinos* and expected the evangelization to lead to that eventually. But Rutilio, especially, felt that this was not the job of the parish and that, besides exposing the pastoral effort to attack, it would risk manipulating the people's faith. He also opposed those who considered reflection on "social reality" the best starting-point for pastoral work. Although he agreed that evangelization must include conscientization, he insisted on starting with the people's religious practice, something more their own, not "imported" from outside, and giving priority to the Gospel over any ideology and to evangelization over politicization.

As Rutilio put it, "We come to put leaven in the dough, not to give them a plan!" He was convinced that the Gospel not only called for radical social change, but was also indispensable to achieve it in a humane way. Others considered him blind to the need for a "scientific analysis" and a revolutionary strategy. In these priorities, the pastoral team followed Rutilio. In fact, in this policy and others, the pastoral strategy of the Aguilares team would spread to other parishes and even influence archdiocesan plans.

It was this general policy that Romero, too, would later follow in relating faith to the social order. But events quickly overtook the team. They had hoped to see peasant solidarity emerge in about three years. Now, after just eight months, they were in the thick of social conflict. Since the massive electoral fraud of March 1972, one could sense mounting unrest around the country, but few could appreciate that these were just the beginnings of a deepening crisis that would shake El Salvador to its foundations and plunge the nation into civil war. The Aguilares team leapt into this vortex without realizing it. Its novel form of evangelization was laying the foundation for the rapid growth of FECCAS, the *campesino* organization. To complicate matters, Jesuit students living in Aguilares, although not part of the pastoral team, were key organizers of FECCAS. The organization built on the base-community structure, siphoning off the most gifted leaders of the parish and rapidly politicizing them. Among Jesuits, this provoked constant clashes which spilled over into the wider community.

By mid-1976 there would be a FECCAS chapter in every hamlet of the parish, and leaders from Aguilares would be traveling around the country promoting the organization and assuming major responsibilities in it. Tilo feared that the political organization would swallow up the base communities. As sacramental practice fell, he insisted that liturgical celebration was necessary to sustain a serious commitment. As the *campesinos* deepened their reflection on the Bible, some found justification in the Old Testament for using violence in their desperate situation. Apocalyptic theology began to appear. FECCAS had no organic links to guerrilla organizations, but the movement offered the *campesinos* a deeper analysis of their plight: capitalism is exploitation; the state is an instrument of the ruling class; the key to history is the class struggle. Tilo felt that the FECCAS were moving too fast and wondered if the evangelization effort had neglected the teaching of the magisterium.

FECCAS developed in two years from a Christian organization for co-operatives to a revolutionary Christian organization and then to a Christian revolutionary organization, growing more independent of the parish at each wrenching stage. Still, they needed the protection of the parish. In the prevailing context, FECCAS could only have grown up under the umbrella of the church. So, even as the organization and the parish team proclaimed their mutual independence, they were one in the eyes of their enemies.

Tensions between FECCAS and the parish team mounted. The parish team complained in 1975 of the "manifest and evident danger of the disintegration of the [parish] work" on account of rash actions which "instrumentalized" the parish for questionable political ends. Rutilio spoke for the parish team: "We don't want to serve as outer cover for a process we disagree with in its steps and its viability." The parish team feared FECCAS would provoke a fatal backlash.

In fact, repression escalated geometrically. The local "security" apparatus had reorganized as a negative reflection of the organization of the parish's Delegates of the Word. Around the country, the socially committed individuals and organizations endured surveillance, searches, calumnies in the media, threats, paramilitary assaults, military raids, jailings, torture, and killings. Rutilio wrote to Archbishop Chávez: "If they kill us or throw us in prison, wonderful! But I pray they don't crush the *campesinos* or our collaborators because of us!" Twice Tilo tried to resign. In 1975 he wanted FECCAS out of parish facilities and refused to host its national convention for 1976. That year brought an outright break between the parish team and the organization. Rutilio forbade one Jesuit working with FECCAS from celebrating Mass publicly in Aguilares for some months.

Through all this, Rutilio's renown grew as he spoke out in the teeth of growing repression. In July 1976, the so-called Conservative Religious Front published a flyer threatening to kill him and other pastors of the vicariate for their supposed partisan politics, for preaching hatred, and for agitating class violence. Rutilio used the occasion to preach about the social demands of the Gospel. Of his accusers he said:

> Let them read the Bible well and slowly . . . they will find Jesus of Nazareth subversive, and most likely they would sign him up with some existing political party here . . . the people, in the great majority *campesinos*, suffer the exploitation of a senseless and reactionary minority which says it calls itself "Catholic" but which is not, because it is unjust, full of greed and lacking in love. To speak these bitter truths to this minority is to really love them, in order that they might be converted and change. To disguise these barbarities is not to love [those who perpetrate] them. It's something like a doctor who, because he doesn't want the patient to suffer, doesn't want to cure him, squeezing a wound full of pus. To love the sick person will be to squeeze the wound so that he be healed and cured. Repent, said Jesus! I am not afraid of anything in defending the [people's] interests, even though that comes to cost me life itself. Giving up one's life for love of one's neighbor just as Jesus did is the greatest blessing that a person can have.

Tilo to his attackers and those like them on making a god of money:

> It is the god money and their interests. They wake up thinking of the almighty name of the god money; they go to bed thinking in the almighty name of the god money, even though thousands of *campesinos* continue *mugrientos*, squalid, anemic and poor. Hypocrites! Stop calling yourselves conservative Catholics, because you are lying!

Recalling how some landowners took great pride in organizing processions of the saints, Tilo reminded them that most of the saints "sealed their lives by martyrdom. But these Catholic landowners, in no way want you to explain to the people the reason that the saint was murdered: they executed him for speaking the truth to someone with power! Parading the saints through the streets—and Jesus himself on Good Friday—doesn't cost anything; but explaining a little about their deaths and the reasons for them—that they won't tolerate."

In his Independence Day homily in 1976, Rutilio recalled that "in the past and even in the present, the religion offered to the people was concerned more with the beyond than with the here and now, more with souls than with the whole person. I never saw any souls walking around." This he saw as a deformation and a grave betrayal of the message of Jesus: "The Reign of God . . . begins in this world which God created for all people equally. And no one will be able to enter the second stage of the Reign of God without an effort to implant it on earth, in justice, in love, and in real brotherhood and sisterhood."

Rutilio declared he was no politician. His only politics was that of the common good: "No one in the world can prohibit me in virtue of some law or decree from seeking the common good of the people: not the pope, not the bishop, no ruler or authority. The priest owes the entire community a spirit of service, unto death if that be necessary."

By 1975 violence and threats were proliferating, and priests were now favorite targets. The president of the country began to denounce "liberationist priests." One such priest, Rafael Barahona, was captured and beaten. In 1976, the government scuttled a modest land reform, six bombs exploded in the Jesuit university, and violent clashes caused two deaths at *campesino* assemblies near Aguilares. Shadow groups denounced "communist priests" in the media. The organized right accused the church, and especially the Jesuits, of directing subversion. The Salvadoran bishops publicly divided over the crisis, some denouncing FECCAS.

Rutilio's old friend, Luis Chávez, had been archbishop for thirty-eight years, but the pressure was too much for him. In January 1977, he offered his resignation. The nuncio announced, to the delight of conservative sectors, that the Vatican would name Bishop Oscar Romero to replace him. Soon after, the rightist organization FARO denounced "preachers of the bloody revolution of hate and violence" and priests who were "little angels with red wings and machine-guns under their cassocks." In one month five priests were tortured or expelled from the country. A member of the oligarchy was kidnapped by guerrillas and his body recovered on 10 February. On 20 February, presidential elections took place. Two days later, Romero was formally installed as archbishop. Rutilio knew that Romero frowned on the Aguilares pastoral adventure; but they were friends and they respected each other. Although deeply disappointed by Romero's appointment, Rutilio nevertheless encouraged others to rally to the new archbishop's side as the church suffered persecution. He personally urged the new archbishop to respond decisively and publicly to the attacks.

The day he was installed, Romero and four other bishops met with the president and other officials, who handed them a list of "subversive priests."

The bishops protested the expulsion of priests without dialogue, but to no avail. When the results of the presidential elections were announced a few days later, thousands occupied Liberty Park protesting fraud. The security forces attacked the protesters in the pre-dawn hours of 27 February, killing one hundred, wounding two hundred, and arresting five hundred. A meeting of clergy, religious, and bishops had been scheduled for the morning of the 28th, and Romero had asked Rutilio Grande to speak on Protestant sects. As accounts of the massacre interrupted the meeting, Romero listened, asked questions. The agenda was scrapped, and Romero then requested all to return to their parishes and welcome those who were in danger. He was making his break with the government.

On 5 March, one week before Rutilio Grande's death, the Bishops' Conference issued a communiqué denouncing not only violations of human rights but also the steep concentration of wealth and land. They proclaimed that the mission of the church was to announce a reign of God that begins here on earth and that the church should stand with the poor in support of concrete means to rectify the injustice of the country. Romero had succeeded in unifying the bishops one last time. The Bishops' Conference would soon become hopelessly polarized.

On 28 January, Mario Bernal, a native of Colombia and pastor of Santa Catarina de Apopa near Aguilares, had been captured and deported. The pastors of the vicariate prevailed on Rutilio to preside at a Mass of protest in Apopa on 13 February. There Rutilio delivered his best-known homily—and very likely sealed his own fate:

> All of us human beings have one common Father. So, all evidently are brothers and sisters. . . . But Cain is an abortion in the Plan of God, and . . . here in this country Cains exist, and they invoke God which is worse. God, the Lord . . . gave us a material world for all without boundaries. That's what Genesis says. It's not a matter of my saying: "I bought half of El Salvador with my money." . . . That is a denial of God! No such right is valid before the majority of the country. The material world is for all without boundaries. So, one common table with long tablecloths for everyone, like this Eucharist. Love . . . sums up all the ethical codes of humanity which Jesus subsumes and surpasses. It is the love of shared fraternity which breaks and throws down every kind of barrier and prejudice, and it has to overcome hatred itself. We are not here on account of hate! We even love the Cains. . . . Love, which is conflictive and which demands . . . moral

violence. I didn't say physical violence . . . I say this for the tape recorders. That is not our violence. That violence is the Word of God, which does violence to us and does violence to society, and which unites us and congregates us, even though they beat us . . . I greatly fear, my dear brothers and sisters, that very soon the Bible and the Gospel will not be able to cross our borders. Only the bindings will reach us because all the pages are subversive. Subversive of sin, of course . . . I greatly fear, brothers and sisters, that if Jesus of Nazareth would return, as before, coming down from Galilee to Judea, that is from Chalatenango to San Salvador, I dare say that with his actions and his preaching, he wouldn't reach . . . Apopa. I believe that they would detain him up there around Guazapa. They would take him prisoner there and put him in jail. [Here someone sabotages the microphone. Rutilio finds a megaphone and continues, to hardy applause] . . . They would take him before Supreme Tribunals as unconstitutional and subversive. . . . They would accuse him of rebellions, a foreign Jew, confusing people with strange and exotic ideas contrary to "democracy." . . . Without a doubt, brothers and sisters, they would crucify him again.

Three weeks later, on Saturday, 12 March, Rutilio and five riders made their way in the parish Safari through the cane fields between Aguilares and El Paisnal, where a Mass was scheduled. A storm of bullets stopped them short, killing Rutilio, Manuel Solorzano (age seventy-two), and Nelson Rutilio Lemus (age fifteen). The killers allowed three young children to run away, terrified, through the cane fields. One subsequently identified his godfather, with known ties to the security forces, as the ringleader of the assassins.

The rich and powerful had committed a tragic error, turning a zealous pastor into a local saint and popular hero. Perhaps the single most important effect of Rutilio's death was its impact on Archbishop Romero. Rutilio, Nelson, and Manuel had been murdered about 5:30 P.M.; Romero arrived in Aguilares, visibly shaken, as Mass was beginning about 10:00 P.M. After the somber liturgy, he convoked a late-night meeting of priests, sisters, and laypeople and asked, in what would become his trademark manner, "What should we do and what can we do as church in response to the death of Father Grande?" He was now ready to take the decisive action that Rutilio had earlier asked of him.

On Monday at the funeral Mass in the cathedral, the archbishop roundly affirmed the pastoral work of Aguilares as a faithful embodiment of Paul VI's *Evangelii Nuntiandi*. Romero gave thanks for these three martyred "co-workers in Christian liberation." As a companion of Rutilio remarked, at that moment, "If he had harbored some doubts about Tilo's pastoral work, these vanished" before his broken body. The three victims were buried in the church at El Paisnal the same day.

During the rest of the week, laypeople, sisters, and priests rallied around Romero in the type of collective work that would characterize the next three years of his ministry. Catholic schools suspended classes for three days of reflection. The archbishop announced that he would attend no government functions until Rutilio's murder had been clarified. The following Sunday all Masses in the archdiocese were canceled except a single Mass at the cathedral. The organized right objected that this would oblige many to "miss Mass." The papal nuncio protested [without merit] that the measure violated canon law, but Romero disagreed and pressed ahead. An estimated one hundred thousand attended the single Mass, perhaps the largest assembly of Salvadorans ever up to that time. Priests hearing confessions recounted that people were returning to the church after many years, moved by the witness of Padre Grande. Romero had been archbishop only one month. But in view of his clashes with the papal nuncio over the single Mass and the persecution, he made a brief visit to Rome to explain his pastoral work to the pope. The secretary of the Congregation of Bishops lectured him, but Pope Paul received him warmly. Violence and persecution of the church escalated. Eight died during 1 May Labor Day clashes. Days later, the archdiocesan printing office was bombed for the second time. A Jesuit was captured, beaten, and expelled. On 11 May, diocesan priest Alfonso Navarro was gunned down along with a young parishioner, apparently in reprisal for the execution of the foreign minister by guerrillas. Flyers began to circulate reading "Be a patriot, kill a priest."

On 19 May, two months after Grande's death, the army occupied Aguilares and cut it off from outside communications as part of what the army called "Operation Rutilio." Witnesses claimed the soldiers killed fifty, brutally mistreating many others, especially if they had a crucifix or a picture of Rutilio in their homes. Hundreds were taken away. The army turned the church into their barracks, machine-gunning the tabernacle. The three remaining Jesuits in Aguilares were deported. When the siege was finally lifted on 19 June, Archbishop Romero returned to celebrate Mass and comfort the community. He told the people:

> You are the image of . . . Christ nailed to the cross and transfixed by a spear. It is the image of all those towns which, like Aguilares, will be

transfixed, will be trampled, but . . . Aguilares is singing the precious refrain of liberation. . . . We suffer with those who are lost, with those who are fleeing and do not know what is happening to their families. . . . We are with those who suffer torture.

It was the first of the great, prophetic homilies of Romero. The five thousand present applauded. After the Mass the congregation filed out in procession toward the square with Romero carrying the Blessed Sacrament. When the National Guard, armed with rifles, threatened to block the procession, the people turned to Romero. He called out, "Keep going!" The guard drew back and the procession moved ahead. Two days later the White Warriors Union threatened to kill all the Jesuits in El Salvador if they did not leave, but the Jesuits made clear their intention to stay and the deadline passed without incident.

The new president was to be inaugurated on 1 July. In the preceding five months, two priests had been killed, two tortured, one beaten, two jailed, four [besides the Jesuits] threatened with death, seven refused reentry to the country, and eight expelled. It was now clear to Romero that the government would undertake no serious investigation. So, in a dramatic break with tradition, he refused to attend the new president's inauguration. Two other bishops did attend, however, including the military vicar, who justified government violence in the interest of "safeguarding public order."

Rutilio's death, and the persecution of which it was a part, had become a sign of contradiction revealing the hearts of many. One week after Rutilio's murder, Cardinal Casariego of Guatemala wrote to his priests warning them to stay out of politics, citing the case of El Salvador where "several priests were expelled from the country [he might have added "and killed"] for departing from their mission and meddling in partisan and sectarian politics." The organized right published these words in all the Salvadoran papers. Archbishop Romero quickly grasped that, once he had taken a stand with the poor and opposed their enemies, he drew the fire of persecution to himself. Now the pious, "orthodox," "nonpolitical" churchpeople, including most of the bishops, abandoned him or even openly opposed him. Some sent negative reports to Rome. During Romero's three years, the Vatican sent three official visitors to investigate his pastoral practice. No such visitors reviewed the work of bishops who supported the military and even neglected their pastoral responsibilities. Romero also discovered, however, that the poor and the great majority of priests and religious, especially those whom he had previously criticized and suspected, rallied to his side.

Eight months after Grande's assassination, the archbishop returned to Aguilares and celebrated the Eucharist in El Paisnal, calling the parish "a marvelous example . . . in the forefront of the Church," all the more important, he said, ". . . because I believe that we have mutilated the Gospel very much; we have tried to live a very comfortable Gospel, without giving up our life. . . . But look how in Aguilares a daring movement has begun of a more committed Gospel . . . it has to do with a very serious commitment to Christ crucified."

The Legacy of Rutilio and Romero

What do Rutilio and Romero say to us? Today the martyrs continue to be good news for the world and for the church even as bad news surrounds us. To the world they are signs of credible love and so of hope amid cynicism and despair. To the church they show how to follow Christ faithfully today. Consider, for example, how Rutilio and Romero exercised leadership in their ministries. Grande the priest and Romero the bishop channeled their personal commitments through these offices. Today, as we witness a kind of "sacerdotalization" of the church, it might feel uncomfortable to emphasize that. We are frequently reminded that the church is not a democracy and left wondering whether it is a tyranny. It is for this very reason that we need to recall how Romero and Grande broke with clerical authoritarianism in favor of broadly consultative and participatory leadership in their ministries without surrendering the teachings of the Gospel or of the church.

How did Rutilio and Romero exercise leadership and authority? Before being sent to Aguilares, Rutilio insisted on team ministry for the parish. At Lumen Vitae in Belgium almost ten years earlier, at a time of personal crisis, he had resolved to break with the authoritarian clerical approach to pastoral ministry in favor of broader participation in decisionmaking and the formation of lay leaders. Aguilares never became a clerical fiefdom. Its pastoral team welcomed hordes of collaborators—and sometimes too many! Rutilio also championed the dignity of women and their active ministry, both in and beyond Aguilares.

As for Romero, at the beginning of his ministry as archbishop, what most impressed many were his frequent appeals for help and advice. Simple poor people treasure the memory of the archbishop explaining a problem to them and asking their personal opinion. Each week a team of advisors helped Romero prepare his Sunday homily. His pastoral letters involved countless meetings and rewritings. For the fourth letter, and also in preparation for the Puebla Conference, he used a written questionnaire to solicit opinions throughout the archdiocese.

This participatory style of leadership was an expression of the fundamental option of both men: the reign of God, integral liberation, God's project of new human beings in a new community. Announcing this good news to the poor was the very heart of their ministry. It gave meaning to the sacraments, preaching, catechism, and popular devotions. The prophetic ministry of Rutilio and Romero shaped the church of the poor, with its support of popular organizations and its martyrs.

The poor, as representatives of Christ, were Romero's fundamental criterion for decisionmaking and for evaluating events. He did not first ask "How will this measure affect the church?" but rather "How will this affect the poor?" On several occasions, he risked the interests of the institutional church in order to stand with the poor. In one of the most politically charged moments of El Salvador's history, Romero ventured an evaluation of the three contending political projects on the basis of what each project offered the poor. He completely rejected the rightist projects of the oligarchy as anti-Christian, "anti-pueblo," idolatry of wealth and power: "The right means precisely social injustice, and it is never just to maintain a rightist orientation."

To the consternation of the left, he did not condemn outright the project of the reformist juntas of 1979–80. He praised their promise of radical change but condemned both the hypocrisy of "reforms bathed in blood" and the way that the Christian Democrats lent a facade to official repression. The reforms, he added, ought not lead to "a capitalist economic model that permits . . . continued accumulation and concentration of wealth in a few hands." Romero did not identify himself, or the church, with any concrete project, but he found more to approve in the still inchoate project of the popular organizations precisely because he saw there "the best, and the most workable translation into political terms of the option for the poor." He favored this project even as he criticized the popular organizations for their frequent sectarianism, the absolutization of politics, dogmatism, violence, and insensitivity to religious values. When a reporter asked what he thought of the left, Romero replied that he did not think of the popular organizations as organizations of the left but rather as organizations of the people. In such a volatile situation, Romero could easily have appealed to the church's neutrality in political matters and safeguarded what some considered the interests of the church. But that would not have served the interests of the poor.

The lesson is still valid. Following the lead of bishops like the late Cardinal Bernardin and Archbishop Weakland, the U.S. bishops made the poor the decisive criterion for evaluating the economy. Today the poor of the world desperately need the church in the United States to apply this criterion to U.S. foreign policy as the U.S. government bullies the United Nations; refuses to recognize a right to food at the World Food Summit in Rome; imposes draconian economic policies on poor countries through the multilateral lending agencies; renews high-tech arms sales to repressive Latin American militaries; legitimizes the brutality of these same militaries at the School of the Americas in Fort Benning, Georgia; competes for the distinction of stingiest foreign-aid donor in the world; and imposes an immoral blockade on the people of Cuba.

The pope has suggested that the Synod of the Americas in Rome this coming November would be an appropriate opportunity for the bishops of both American continents to review North-South relations, which includes the problem of the external debt, which stands today at $1,000 for every man, woman, and child in Latin America and which continues to straitjacket the economies of Africa and Latin America. The church's credibility depends on whether its future leadership will stand by the defenseless in the spirit of Romero and Rutilio. Clouds certainly darken the horizon. Church leadership often seems to be retreating rather than advancing in this respect. Church leaders who opt for the poor are suspected and investigated; those who opt for prestige and personal power are frequently promoted. Some want to forget the legacy of Romero and a generation of martyrs. Romero is never mentioned in episcopal documents in El Salvador, for example. Nor was he mentioned during the papal Mass there. But it will be difficult to keep the martyrs in their tombs.

At the time of the pope's visit to El Salvador, our Pastoral Center at the Central American University (UCA) was besieged by reporters who wanted us to confirm stories that seemed to have been written before they left Europe or North America. The outline went like this: "The pope visited Central America in 1983 when Marxism threatened to take over society and liberation theology threatened to take over the church. Now Marxism is dead, and liberation theology lives only in the brains of aging theologians." Well, I can't speak for Marxism, but the diagnosis regarding liberation theology and, by implication, the prophetic church of the poor, seems to me, to paraphrase Mark Twain, greatly exaggerated.

We at the UCA directed reporters' attention to a recent survey of religion in El Salvador conducted by our university some months before. Pollsters asked [Salvadoran] Catholics, should the church "get involved in social conflicts"? Forty-eight percent responded "yes," a large plurality (since 14 percent had no opinion) representing a 10 percent increase since 1988. Catholics were then asked if the church "ought to prefer the poor." Sixty percent said "yes," up from 43 percent seven years before. When asked if Archbishop Romero should be canonized, 50 percent of Catholics said "yes" (with 20 percent expressing no opinion), more than double the percentage (22 percent) in 1988. In addition, 83 percent of all Salvadorans felt that the newly appointed archbishop ought to denounce social injustice and promote action to eradicate poverty. Forty-four percent of Catholics agreed that good Christians could vote for a party of the left, versus 38 percent who said "no" (16 percent expressed no opinion). By contrast, 29 percent of Protestants (mostly from Pentecostal groups) said "yes" and 56 percent "no" (15 percent had no opinion). Keep in mind that many people would be fearful to express these majority and plurality views in El Salvador.

The responses demonstrate how a high percentage of Salvadorans now take for granted the fundamental convictions of the church of the poor and liberation theology. Even unbelievers express indignation at the archdiocese's present retreat from social responsibilities. After thirty-eight years of Archbishop Chávez, three of Romero, and fifteen years of Rivera Damas, even most unbelievers consider failure to stand by the poor as dereliction of duty on the part of the church. These convictions have taken deep root because, far from having been imposed by elites, they feed on the faith of the poor themselves and also, of course, because they are sealed in blood. Archbishop Romero prophesied that, even if he were killed, his word would remain. And so it has—not only his spoken word but also his martyrdom, which Bishop Casadáliga has called his greatest homily. I am convinced—and this is no poetic exaggeration—that Romero exercises more real influence in El Salvador today than any person walking around "in the flesh." He is a constant point of reference—in classes, homilies, and ordinary conversations.

To the surprise of some, younger Salvadorans, the great majority in this young country, are appropriating the martyrs' legacy, as they have demonstrated at commemorative celebrations and during the pope's visit. This legacy is alive and well in so many homes and parishes and Catholic schools thanks in great part to those key formers of youth, the women religious. Like all young people today, young Salvadorans, even in their poverty, feel the tug of consumer society. But partly because of the inroads of liberal culture, they are also developing an increasingly critical consciousness. Like their peers elsewhere, young Salvadorans reject the old hypocrisies and authoritarianism in the church. But this does not mean they want out. It means they respond to a consistent and credible love. The martyrs have demonstrated such love. As Jon Sobrino says, a credible love has its own efficacy, because it inspires others to "carry on the cause that was expressed in that love." In the South as in the North, the church of the future will either stand with the poor in a credible love like this, or else it will be standing with fewer and fewer people altogether.

Walbert Bühlmann has written of the Third Church, meaning the church of the Third World. The First Church is the church of the East, of Asia and Eastern Europe: the Second Church is the church of the West, which dominated missionary activity and with it the onetime mission lands. But this dominance is passing. Two-thirds of Christians, including 63 percent of Catholics, now live in the poor South and comprise the Third Church. About thirty years ago, the demographic center of gravity in the Catholic Church shifted from the North to the South. More Catholics now live in Latin America than in Europe and North America combined. And these local churches have come into their majority. In time for the third millennium, as Karl Rahner noted, the Church has finally become a global church. The Third Church invites the global church to become ever more the "church of the poor." Through this Third Church the poor of the earth invite the whole church to correct rather fundamental defects in our way of being church that reach back at least to the Constantine settlement, when the church became allied with state power. That formula has been modified and reformed over the centuries, but today the Third Church invites the whole church to pact a new alliance with the powerless as Jesus did and from there to announce a credible "salvation" for all, a reign of God which begins here and is eternal life, new human beings living in communion with God and one another.

The First and Second Churches had their "Fathers," their Chrysostoms and Augustines (and their Mothers, too, whose teaching has not come down to us); and they had their doctors, their Aquinases and Teresas of Avila. It is hardly fashionable to speak of Fathers of the Church today; but this "Third Church" invites us, I think, to speak analogously of "Fathers" as in the past. The Third Church may well have more Mothers than Fathers, but Romero, analogically speaking, will certainly be one of its fathers. Some years ago, I received a letter from a Jesuit in Peru who had just read Romero's homilies. "He was not invented by the left," my friend exclaimed. He was amazed at the depth and richness of Romero's thought. Bishop Pedro Casadáliga of Brazil has said that "The history of the Church in Latin America divides into two parts: before and after Romero." But Romero's witness echoes far beyond Latin America. Romero will deserve, I believe, to be recognized as a genuine Doctor of the Church of the next millennium, a doctor of the church of the poor, which is the only church with the right to call itself Christian, the only church that can be everyone's church, and so the only church with the right to call itself Catholic.

It is difficult to speak a credible word about God today, and perhaps that is how it should be. Before he was tortured and killed in Bolivia in 1980, Luis Espinal said, "Whoever does not have the courage to speak on behalf of human beings has no right to speak of God." Romero could speak a credible word about God because, for him, as he said in paraphrasing Irenaeus of Lyons, "Gloria Dei, pauper vivens," the glory of God is that the poor have life. Rutilio, Romero, and others like them speak a credible word about God because they gave witness to God's own compassion for those who are suffering. Rutilio fell, not at the altar, but on the altar. So tonight we can apply the thoughts of the Spaniard Jose Marta Valverde to both Rutilio and Romero—and by extension, to many like them:

> Dark centuries ago, it is told, a bishop died by order of a king, spattering the chalice with his blood to defend the freedom of the church from the secular might. Well enough, surely. But since when has it been told that a bishop fell at the altar not for the freedom of the church, but simply because he took sides with the poor—because he was the mouth of their thirst for justice crying to heaven.

> When has such a thing been told? Perhaps not since the beginning, when Someone died the death of a subversive and a slave.

8

Archbishop Romero's Challenge to U.S. Universities

(1990)

JOSEPH NANGLE, O.F.M.

The Cathedral of San Salvador is the best place to go for a reflection on the life and death and impact of Archbishop Oscar Romero. One should enter the building through the main doorway, from the central plaza where they tried to hold his funeral but could not because the army fired on the mourners.

This is the way I experienced it shortly after Romero's death. I walked up the aisle of a drab, unfinished church made of rough cement walls and tin roofing. The floor was a dark gray tile, colored thus by the grime from the streets outside. Pigeons flew about the open rafters. The benches were worn and scarred.

Ahead was the main altar, where stood Archbishop Romero's chair and where hung his coat of arms with the motto *sentir con la iglesia*—"feel with the church." The left transept was a nondescript eucharistic chapel. The right transept held the tomb of Oscar Arnulfo Romero Goldámez, archbishop of San Salvador from 22 February 1977 until his assassination on 24 March 1980.

The Cathedral of San Salvador was where the archbishop literally and figuratively lived out his three years as pastor of the Salvadoran people; it was where, Sunday after Sunday, with increasing insistence, he called for an end to the economic, social, and military fratricide that afflicted his people. The cathedral especially was where he spoke for those who had no voice in that society: the orphans, the widows, and the dispossessed. It is where they hurriedly carried his coffin when the military began to fire on his funeral Mass. It is where the visitor saw every day a continuous, spontaneous vigil conducted by every segment of Salvadoran society: men and women; old, middle-aged, and young; well-to-do and poor—especially the poor, always the poor. They entered in ones and twos all day long to say a prayer, light a candle, leave a flower, place a written petition at the grave of Monseñor, their pastor, friend, protector, and martyr.

More symbolically, but no less in reality, the Cathedral of San Salvador stood as a monument to Archbishop Romero's clear and unyielding conviction that decisions must be made on the basis of how the poor will be affected. He would not permit the cathedral to be finished, he said, while the poor lacked the bare necessities of life.[1]

This cathedral—sacrament, symbol, and actualization of Romero's firmest conviction—portrayed for me his message for the church of the United States, indeed for the church in the entire affluent world. This shepherd not only took a personal option for the poor, he also institutionalized that option in the Archdiocese of San Salvador during his three years as its pastor. It was entirely fitting that the *sede*—the seat—of the Salvadoran church, its metropolitan cathedral, would not be completed while the poor remained unattended. That rude church witnesses to Romero's and his entire archdiocese's preferential option for the poor. That, for me, is this martyr's word to us.

In his first letter to the newly elected Pope John Paul II, on 7 November 1978, Romero wrote, "I [have] believed it a duty to take a positive stand in defense of my church and, on the part of the church, at the side of the oppressed and abused people."

Romero's famous Sunday homilies, we are told, were based both on Scripture and on the accounts of the human tragedies recounted to him throughout the previous week by the victims of the multifaceted war waged against the poor. On Sunday Archbishop Romero would read from scraps of paper pressed on him by suffering people or written by himself in his countless daily interviews with the victims. Then he would offer his reflections on the current situation, using the scriptures of the day as inspiration.

Once Romero had seen the privileged place which the poor occupy in salvation history, his mind and heart and soul locked onto that truth with a rigor that was truly prophetic. Both personally and as a personification of the Salvadoran church, Archbishop Romero took his cue from the truth which the poor are—not because they are saints but because "theirs is the kingdom of God."

Not even the divisions within the Salvadoran hierarchy, occasioned by Romero's unshakable faith in the poor, could sway him. Theologian Jon Sobrino tells us that the archbishop "put fidelity to his apostolate to the poor before the anguish of disunion."

And the poor knew of his personal and institutionalized option for them. Father James Brockman, S.J., in his revised work *Romero: A Life,* tells us that a *campesino* community gave the archbishop permission to attend the Latin American Bishops' general meeting at Puebla, Mexico, early in 1979. In addition, the community sent eighty dollars for their pastor's expenses. A cabdriver in San Salvador recognized the archbishop in the adjoining car at a stoplight shortly after the archdiocesan radio station YSAX had been blown up. In typical Latino fashion, the cabbie reached across and handed Romero two dollars *"para la radio, Monseñor"* ("for the radio, Bishop").

This way of being church, this identification with the little ones on a personal and structural level, this institutional option for the poor is, I believe, the legacy and challenge of Oscar Arnulfo Romero to us, both as persons and, just as important, as institutions.

Let me now turn to another martyrdom, which took place at the end of the decade of the 1980s—that of the six Jesuit faculty members of the University of Central America, together with their two women co-workers, Elba Julia Ramos and her daughter, Celinda Maricet. While the Jesuits' option for the poor went back before the three years of Romero's archbishopric, Ignacio, Juan Ramon, Segundo, Armando, Ignacio, and Joaquin were greatly influenced by the archbishop's faith in the poor. Listen to Jon Sobrino, the theologian who formed part of that academic community and who escaped martyrdom on 16 November 1989, perhaps in God's providence to be able to tell the story:

I believe that for [my brothers], for me, and so many others, Archbishop Romero was a Christ for our time, and like Christ, a sacrament of God. To come into contact with Archbishop Romero was like coming into contact with God . . . trying to follow Archbishop Romero was like following Jesus today in El Salvador. This is what my brothers wanted to do. After all, Romero was God's most precious gift to us all in these times.

Romero, the six Jesuits, and their women co-workers will, I believe, remain for-ever joined in the martyrology of El Salvador. Romero's option for the poor, institutionalized in the archdiocese, was the Jesuits' option as well, institution-alized in the university. Just as Romero was killed at the beginning of the decade for standing with the poor, so the Jesuits suffered martyrdom for the same reason at its end.

Father Theodore Hesburgh, C.S.C., in an address at Seton Hall some years ago, said the following: "The most important fact about the Catholic university is that it accepts the truth that God has spoken to [hu]mankind in the Old and New Testaments, that the Son of God has entered history as the Son of Mary, and that Christ the Lord has spoken too, has given us his Gospel, the good news."

Father Hesburgh's affirmation of faith lived institutionally in and through the Catholic center of higher education was taken a step further by the Central American University Jesuits. They moved their entire university to view life through the optic of the poor. That optic became the university's way of seek-ing truth.

Once again, Jon Sobrino speaking of his martyred brothers:

They killed these Jesuit academics for having made of the university an efficacious instrument for the defense of the masses of the people, for hav-ing become a critical conscience in a sinful society and the creative con-science of a different society for the future—the utopia of God's reign on behalf of the poor. They killed them for having tried to make a university truly Christian. They killed them because the Jesuits believed in a God of the poor, and they determined to bring forth this faith in and through the university.

Years earlier Father Ignacio Ellacuría, rector of that university and one of those martyred there, said in an address at Santa Clara University in California:

A Christian-inspired university focuses all its academic activity according to what it means to make a Christian preferential option for the poor. . . . The university should become science for those who have no science, the clear voice of those who have no voice, the intellectual support of those whose very reality makes them true and right and reasonable, even though this sometimes takes the form of having nothing, but who cannot call upon academic reasons to justify themselves. . . . Our university has modestly tried to adopt this difficult and conflictive course.

There can be no doubt about why Archbishop Romero and the Jesuit faculty at the University of Central America saw the need for a personal and institutional option for the poor. The plight of the have-nots remains as the single worst scandal of our times—one which Archbishop Romero and the Jesuit martyrs saw clearly. By any measure I believe we find it to be true, even though the measurements almost defy comprehension. In concentrating here on this well-known yet always surprising scandal, we may be more inclined to take seriously Romero's message to us.

There are a hundred million human beings who live today on sidewalks, garbage dumps, and under bridges. At the same time the world has 157 individuals who are billionaires and some two million millionaires. Four hundred million persons are undernourished to the point of stunted growth, mental retardation, and death today in our world. At the same time, $5 billion are spent each year on dieting to reduce the amount of calories taken in by an overfed world. In Latin America, the per capita income has dropped by 9 percent in the past ten years, while wealthy nations have tripled their per capita income in the past forty years. Today 1.2 billion persons live in absolute poverty, that is, they lack basic biological needs—food, housing, and clothing. At the same time the nations of the world in 1988 spent trillions of dollars each year on the means of warfare. Poverty is widely feminized—women are more likely to be poor; in the world's worst-off countries, female illiteracy is 38 percent higher than that of men.

The so-called Third World, actually two-thirds of the world, owes fully one-half of their gross national products to First World banks and governments. Former Tanzanian president Julius Nyerere asked the question, "Must we starve our children to pay our debts?" That question has now been answered in practice, and the answer has been "yes." Hundreds of thousands of the underdeveloped world's children have given their lives to pay the debts of their countries, and many millions more are still paying the interest with their malnourished minds and bodies.

In our own country, the richest in the world, the panorama is as grim comparatively. More than fifty-one million Americans live below the poverty line. One-fifth of all U.S. children—one in every five—are growing up in poverty.

The world's poor are caught by forces at the local, national, and global levels that combine to form a three-tiered trap. At the local level, these include skewed patterns of access to land and other assets, physical weakness, and heightened susceptibility to disease as well as powerlessness against corrupt institutions. These are reinforced at the national level by innumerable policies—from tax laws to the structure of development investment—that neglect the poor or discriminate against them. And at the global level, the poor are held down by the devastating combination of oppressive debt burdens, high interest rates, falling export prices, and rising capital flight. Poverty in the world of the poor is like a set of Chinese boxes: within the walls of each box lies an even more deprived group. The poor understand full well the stratification of their world into layers of power, influence, and wealth, and they describe it in pointed terms. In the slums of Calcutta, they differentiate between three-meals-a-day people, two-meals-a-day people, and one-meal-a-day people. In northern Bangladesh, villagers speak of "those who sit and eat, and those who work."

To complicate further this nearly incomprehensible situation, poverty is becoming an increasingly environmental phenomenon. The poor suffer disproportionately from environmental damage caused by the better off—and the poor have become a major cause of ecological decline themselves. As they are pushed to marginal lands, they raze plots in the rain forests, plow steep slopes, and overgraze fragile rangeland.

One could go on and on with these numbing statistics and observations. For me, however, a woman I know named Olga Valencia makes all the charts and graphs and comparisons understandable. Olga is one of the one hundred million homeless, one of the four hundred million hungry; her income has dropped at least 9 percent (probably much more) in the past ten years; she embodies the feminization of poverty in her illiteracy, her physical weakness, susceptibility to disease, powerlessness against corrupt institutions. She and all her sisters suffer from the drop in export prices imposed on their native Peru and the rising capital flight there. Olga's environment has deteriorated—the air she breathes, the water she drinks, the very soil under her feet now pose a threat to her life.

I met Olga Valencia some twenty years ago when she already had borne too many children for her undernourished body to nurture. I met her when her oldest son, nine-year-old Jose, was killed by a hit-and-run driver as the lad was returning home with a pot of food he had begged for the family's evening meal. We struggled for three days just to get Jose buried. Over the years, Olga has dictated letters to me, on one occasion telling me of the second son, Vicente, who at twenty years of age was a real help to his mother and siblings.

One day Vincente was taken to the hospital with a fever, and when Olga went to visit him a few days later she was told simply, brutally, "*ha muerto*"—"he died." She has written of her husband's increasing alcoholism and eventual desertion of the family out of his own despair over their situation. I visited Olga last year and found her living in the very same kind of shack as twenty years ago, with two lovely teenaged daughters, about whom she worries constantly, and a younger son who is severely retarded.

Olga puts a face and a voice on impersonal and overwhelming statistics. She brings to life for me the fact that "the poor" have names, are persons—a lesson that Jesus tried to teach when he gave a name to just one person in all his parables: Lazarus, the man who sat outside the rich man's gate unnoticed and unattended. Olga Valencia personifies all of the people for whom Archbishop Romero and the Jesuit academics opted personally and institutionally.

This, then, I believe, is the challenge of Archbishop Romero: that we make of our institutions visible signs of God's own preference for the poor: as often as you did/did not do it to one of these, the least of my brothers or sisters, you did/did not do it to me. Specifically Catholic universities are called by this saint of the Americas to be an institutionalized option for the Olga Valencias. Our universities in a unique way have it within their power to make that historic and efficacious option which the underdeveloped world awaits from Catholic America. Given the talent and resources of these institutions, such an option can mean, literally, the continuation or the termination of this scandal called poverty.

Look, for example, at Notre Dame in the light of such a possible option: it draws its student body from virtually all the states of this country and from many foreign countries; it is ranked among the ten top business schools in the nation and one of the top ten colleges and universities represented by graduates among U.S. business and industrial leaders; it has the largest Catholic academic press in the world; it has been enormously successful in encouraging the development of strong moral character among students; and it ranks in the top twenty-five among all American colleges and universities in the size of its endowment. The listing of Notre Dame's power and potential goes on and on.

Other Catholic centers of higher education fall into line behind Notre Dame to form an immense reservoir of potential and goodwill. In a very recent survey of 134 Catholic colleges and universities, fully 74 percent of all participants, including presidents, academic officers, student affairs officers, and students themselves, indicated that their institutions are making considerable, even great, efforts to cultivate values. In judging Catholic tradition as a guide to value development, 68 percent said that its impact is very important. Our schools of higher learning are really trying to fulfill their calling as Catholic/Christian centers.[2]

Remarkable efforts are made to bring the awareness of a poor and suffering world to Christian campuses. In his introductory essay for the Bulletin of Information 1989–90, Father Edward Malloy writes, "The conviction that scientific research cannot reveal the purpose of man's existence or decide the great moral questions of our time has led the university to commit itself to awakening in its students a sense of the importance of values and the moral responsibilities of caring for others and working for the betterment of society."

To that end, Notre Dame sponsors efforts like Big Brothers/Big Sisters programs, a council for the retarded and neighborhood study help programs, a chapter of Amnesty International, a World Hunger Coalition. Off campus the university sponsors the Appalachian seminar, the summer service projects in inner-city and rural poverty areas, the Urban Plunge, the social concerns seminar in Washington, D.C., and the foreign study program—to name just a few of many dozens of service programs. Many of these initiatives come from the Center for Social Concerns. Latin American/North American Church Concerns (LANACC) also sponsors an annual lecture series commemorating the death of Archbishop Romero.

There is goodwill—there are remarkable initiatives—aimed at bringing to a university of privilege an awareness of a poor and suffering world. The results are impressive: 71 percent of Notre Dame students engage in some form of community service during their college years, and 9 percent devote a full year or more of social service to the less fortunate.

And yet, as Jesus said to the rich young man, looking at him with love, "There is still something lacking in you." What Archbishop Romero and the Jesuit academics did was not only done on a personal, individual level, but an institutional one as well. Translated to every Catholic-Christian institution, diocese, parish school, and religious order, Romero and the Jesuits challenge boards of trustees, campus ministry, and all academic life. The question to each of the departments of the great universities is this: Has the institution become "science for those who have no science, the clear voice of those who have no voice, the intellectual support of those whose very reality makes them true and right and reasonable . . . but who cannot call upon academic reasons to justify themselves?" In a word, are Christian universities institutions of good news to the poor?

It would take more time than humanly possible to spell out all of the implications of this vision, and of these questions. I am clearly not equipped to do this, but those like Romero in his archdiocese and the Jesuits at UCA have the expertise to incarnate this call. Nevertheless, let me cite two examples to suggest the kind of university which the Romero-inspired challenge signifies.

I am told that Notre Dame's board of trustees stated that its principal overriding concern upon receiving a huge cash windfall from the sale of the rights to televise football games was to ensure that the money would assist underprivileged students who wish to attend the university. One might ask many questions about big-time football and network television, as well as about the huge sums of money involved therein in light of an institutionalized option for the poor here at Notre Dame. But the fact remains that institutionally, in its board of trustees, the university clearly sees this matter in light of needy students. Such a conviction on the part of the board goes beyond a personal option for the poor. It is a sign that the trustees as a body demand that the institution pay attention and promote young men and women who otherwise would have no voice, who otherwise would lack intellectual support. Such a posture by the board of trustees affects the university as a whole—it is a fine example of an institutionalized option for the poor.

Another example: Robert Rodes, professor at Notre Dame's School of Law, approaches his discipline through the optic of the poor. Professor Rodes asks how it is that graduates of the law school—of any law school—will generously accept pro-bono cases for the poor which often arise from those very lawyers' defense of powerful interests. His disquiet over a legal system stacked against the poor is translated into the Notre Dame classroom and is exactly what the Jesuit academics in Central America saw as their whole university's approach: "They made of the university an efficacious instrument for the defense of the masses of the people." Can, then, the entire law school, the School of Business, the faculties of the social sciences, engineering, the theology and philosophy departments, the liturgies, prayers, counseling services, administration, and alumni—in a word all that is a Catholic-Christian university—be placed at the service of suffering humanity? That, I believe, is the lasting challenge which Oscar Romero lays at our doorstep. The overwhelming problems of our brothers and sisters, encompassed in the word "poverty," require nothing less than the full attention of our Catholic colleges and universities.

Let me offer by way of conclusion some unsettling reflections in the form of two quotations—one from Archbishop Romero and the other from Jon

Sobrino. Both speak of the need for institutional as well as personal conversion; both mention how they understand conversion happening; and both speak of the danger which every institution faces of neglecting the grace of conversion.

From Archbishop Romero's second pastoral letter of 6 August 1977:

Christians are aware of the radical "no" that God pronounces over our sins of omission. The church is here speaking not only of the conversion that others ought to bring about in their lives, but is speaking in the first instance of its own conversion. This awareness of its own need for conversion is historically something very new, though it was said of the church in the past that it always had to be reformed. The pressure for this conversion came not only when the church looked inward at itself, with its defects and sins, but also when the church looked outward at the sins of the world. The church has regained the basic attitude for conversion, which is to turn toward those who are especially lowly, poor and weak.

Like Christ, we should have pity on the multitudes weighed down with hunger, misery and ignorance. We want to fix a steady gaze on those who still lack the help they need to achieve a way of life worthy of human beings. It is in this encounter with the world of the poor that one finds the most pressing need for conversion. It is the love of Christ that urges us on, that makes a clear demand upon us when we are faced with a brother or sister in need.

From Jon Sobrino's reflections on his martyred brother Jesuits:

They were very much aware that a university is also threatened by sinfulness, that it can serve the anti-kingdom, or more particularly, it can reinforce through the professionals it produces and through its social position the unjust structures in a society. Not only can a university do this, but it frequently does and introduces sin into society. A Christian-inspired university must above all be a converted university. Conversion means putting all its social weight through its specific instrument—rational knowledge—at the service of the oppressed majorities.

One last word, one final call from the saint of the Americas. Addressing Christian political leaders, capitalists, specialists, and professionals in one of his most famous homilies, Archbishop Romero stated:

You have the key to the solution. But the church gives you what you cannot have by yourselves: hope, the optimism to struggle, the joy of knowing that there is a solution, that God is our Father and keeps on urging us. God needed persons to take the paralytic up to the roof and lower him before Christ so that he could cure him. Christ and God . . . want also to have stretcher-bearers, people to help pick up that paralytic called the nation, or society—so that with human hands, with human solutions, with human ideas, we can put him down before Christ, who is the only one who can say "I have seen your faith. Get up and walk."

NOTES

1. The cathedral stood just as Fr. Nangle describes it throughout the tenure of Monsignor Romero and that of his successor, Archbishop Rivera y Damas. The current prelate, Archbishop Saenz Lacalle, subsequently completed extensive renovations.

2. *Sharing Faith across the Hemisphere* (Washington, D.C.: United States Catholic Conference, 1997) reports that academic commitment to Latin America, while far from optimum, is nevertheless substantial—and growing. Of the seventy-one colleges and universities that responded to the NCCB's Catholic College and University Survey, 18.2 percent rated their support of Latin America as "very good," compared to 7.5 percent in 1980–89. The respondents reported major growth in human support: an increase of more than 400 percent in the number of students and 600 percent in the number of faculty who spend time in Latin America, relative to the numbers of the pre-Romero 1970s. Additionally, 83 percent reported "greater" or "much greater" institutional commitment to social change; 73.4 percent reported greater or much greater sensitivity to social justice; and 56.9 percent reported greater or much greater prayer/liturgical concerns. In terms of specific contributions in Latin America, 49.1 percent offer graduate programs; 49.1 percent consistently support other academic programs; 69 percent send students to Latin America; 60.7 percent send faculty or administrators; 36.4 percent send priests; 38.2 percent send sisters or brothers; 42.6 percent make financial contributions; 17.6 percent support diocesan projects; and 7.5 percent adopt a diocese or parish.

Afterword
The Ongoing Legacy of Archbishop Romero

JUAN E. MÉNDEZ AND ROBERT S. PELTON, C.S.C.

Juan E. Méndez—
It is indeed an honor to be asked to participate in this book, by which the Notre Dame community remembers the legacy of Mons. Oscar Arnulfo Romero and preserves it as an example for the future of Catholicism in a world of conflict and injustice. It is an undeserved honor and, for that reason, it is also a very challenging task. It is difficult to contribute some thoughts that would do justice to the depth and insight of the pieces collected in this book.

For years, the Romero lectures have been a highlight of Notre Dame's commitment to scholarship and service. They have also been the most visible way in which American Catholics ensure that the legacy of the archbishop of San Salvador is preserved and that his example endures. For that, Fr. Robert Pelton, C.S.C., and the editors of this book deserve much credit. As the director of the Center for Civil and Human Rights at Notre Dame, I feel duty-bound to join them in this task, in spite of my limited familiarity with Romero's significance for the history of the Church and with his theological contributions. I shall comment from the modest perspective of a Latin American who belongs to the human rights movement in that part of the world, an identity that instantly classifies me as one of the many, perhaps millions, who owe an immense debt of gratitude to Archbishop Romero.

Thanks largely to Archbishop Romero, it can be legitimately said that in Latin America the Catholic Church stands by the poor and oppressed and defends the most vulnerable persons from the abuses of power. To be sure, the record is not uniformly similar to that of the Archdiocese of San Salvador in the 1970s and 1980s. (After Romero's murder in 1980 his successor, Monsignor Arturo Rivera y Damas, continued his work with similar dedication.) Even in El Salvador there were priests who sided with the military and with the death squads lending them cover and political support. In countries like Argentina, Guatemala, and Peru, some bishops also followed Romero's example, in some instances also having to lay down their lives in the service of human rights. As an institution, however, the Church in those countries and elsewhere in Latin America too often looked passively on while the tragedy of massacres, disappearances, and torture unfolded.

Romero's example, fortunately, has not been an isolated heroic act. Well-known church leaders like McGrath in Panama, Gerardi in Guatemala, Ruiz in Mexico, Arns, Casadáliga, and Camara in Brazil, Proaño in Ecuador, and Silva Enríquez in Chile, among others, have held high the banner of the defense of the rights of the human person even under the worst conditions. Thanks to the example they and Romero set, today the Church in Cuba, Venezuela, Colombia, Honduras, Guatemala, and Mexico is properly regarded as a stalwart defender of the poor and of human dignity.

Although the recent appointments from Rome have favored more orthodox leaders, the defense of human rights has been continued. This is in part because human rights are not the province of liberal or progressive thinkers; undeniably, the human rights canon and doctrine are broad enough to include persons with varying positions within the ideological spectrum. But at least in Latin America this is true in large part also because the legacy of Archbishop Romero lives on in the hearts of Catholic men and women, religious or laypersons, and that legacy constitutes a demand that must be met. In fact, defense of the poor and oppressed becomes a special Latin American way of being Christian.

Robert S. Pelton, C.S.C.—
Monsignor Romero's legacy lives in the social, political, and legal spheres as well. His works and his martyrdom produced an enormous groundswell of support for many vital initiatives based upon his insights into the needs of his flock, the mission of the Church, and the teachings of Christ. Following his

death, his initiatives were carried through by his successors, especially Archbishop Rivera y Damas and the Jesuits at the University of Central America.

One of his most significant legacies is reflected in the 1992 Peace Agreement that was signed between the government of El Salvador and the opposition forces. Although the agreement was formally ratified twelve years after Monsignor Romero's martyrdom, he had both anticipated and paved the way for three of its most fundamental human rights issues:

1. The dissolution of the three branches of the security forces and the creation of a new civilian police force. In his fourth pastoral letter, "The Church amid the National Crisis," Archbishop Romero committed to seeking profound structural changes in military and police powers and practices, and he vigorously denounced "the absolutization of National Security."

2. The extremely significant change in the status of the FMLN from that of guerrilla force to that of a major political party deeply involved in national politics. Romero's third pastoral letter, "The Church and Popular Political Organization," emphasized that violence and revolutionary sentiments were arising from the exclusion of *campesinos*, workers, and other average citizens from a government that listened only to the wealthiest and most powerful elite. Throughout the final years of his life, Romero championed the right of the Salvadoran people to form social, economic, and political organizations that would help them to secure their rights through peaceful means.

3. The government's commitment to carrying out reforms in land distribution after the war. In "The Absolutization of Wealth and Private Property," Romero wrote: "In our country, idolatry [of wealth and privilege] is at the root of structural and repressive violence." In countless writings and homilies, he emphasized that the God who created the world for his children also created a "social mortgage" upon land and other resources—a responsibility to share his gift fairly and equitably with our brothers and sisters.

By being a major force for human rights the Latin American Church has contributed enormously to the growth and expansion of the human rights movement in that region. Today, there are literally thousands of organizations of civil society dedicated to defending the rights of others. Some of them document on violations and report them, along the lines of the method pioneered by Socorro Jurídico, the organization founded by Monsignor Romero. Others are set up mostly to use the courts and other state institutions in the service of the public interest, and to change policies and practice through litigation on behalf of the poor. There are some that concentrate on freedom of expression, and there are many dedicated to the rights of the child. A large number of groups engage in education, both on promoting the effectiveness of the right to education and expanding and disseminating the possibilities of human rights education. It is significant that the most important regional organization dedicated to human rights education, the Inter-American Institute on Human Rights of San José, Costa Rica, is now under the direction of Mr. Roberto Cuéllar, the Salvadoran lawyer to whom Mons. Romero entrusted the work of Socorro Jurídico in the fateful late 1970s. Very appropriately, Mr. Cuéllar was asked by Notre Dame to deliver the Romero lecture in the year 2000.

Unquestionably, not all human rights work in Latin America is Church-inspired. And it must be remembered that on issues regarding nondiscrimination on grounds of sexual preference, reproductive rights, and sexual abuse of children entrusted to deviant priests, some NGOs and the Church have been on a collision course. Significantly, however, the legacy of Monsignor Romero and other Catholic leaders has imbued Catholic and non-Catholic human rights organizations with a spirit of tolerance and respect for diversity, so that those differences do not result in clashes and do not prevent the human rights movement from acting together on larger issues of truth and justice.

It took more than ten years after Romero's death for the warring factions in El Salvador to put an end to the conflict. With the assistance of the international community, the peace process itself became a tribute to Romero's vision. It included on-site civilian monitoring of human rights performance by both parties, much along the lines of what Socorro Jurídico and its network of parish priests, religious communities of men and women, and lay activists had tried to do earlier. The establishment of civilian monitoring even before a cease-fire was part of this bold vision, and it has become a model for conflict resolution in other parts of the world. The peace process also included a Truth Commission and an Ad Hoc Commission to examine the files of hundreds of notorious military leaders, many of whom were not allowed to stay in the ranks of the armed forces because of their behavior towards the rights of the citizenry. The agreements also included internationally monitored and assisted efforts to reform the judiciary, the police, and the security forces, and the creation of new institutions, like the ombudsman's office, designed to provide more effective remedies to the victims of abuse.

El Salvador has retained a peaceful commitment to democracy in the decade since the war ended, and many things have improved there, most notably the attitude and performance of a military establishment now under the authority of a democratized civilian government. Undoubtedly, Salvadorans have worked for this under the inspiration of Monsignor Romero. But it would be a mistake to label El Salvador fully democratic while many features of what Romero condemned and sought to change are still there. For one, a shameful blanket amnesty was passed right after the report of the Truth Commission, so that all of the war crimes and crimes against humanity committed during the long conflict remain mired in impunity. Indeed, the murderers of Monsignor Romero have not been brought to justice. There is also no justice for the 1989 murder of six Jesuit priests, their landlady, and her teenage daughter; or for the assassination of the four American churchwomen in December 1980; or for the massacre of dozens of unarmed civilians, mostly elderly, women, and children, in the hamlet of El Mozote. In fact, the Salvadoran government, dominated by ARENA, the party founded in part by those who had Romero killed, holds fast to the notion that total impunity for these crimes is necessary for "reconciliation." There may be peace in El Salvador, but to deserve the label of democratic the state must find a way to break the cycle of impunity and allow the full truth to be told about the atrocities of those years, and afford their victims a full measure of justice and reparations.

The powerful life and untimely death of Oscar Arnulfo Romero compel Salvadorans and Latin Americans to confront their past and to take an honest look at the failings of their societies and regimes. But they also call upon the citizens of the United States to examine the country's foreign policy and see if it fosters democracy in the region and protects and promotes human rights for all peoples. It is significant that the actions by Romero that his killers considered the ultimate provocation were directly related to the policies of the United States. One was his "order" to the Salvadoran military to stop the killing of innocents, at a time when the United States was so afraid of "losing" El Salvador that we were ready to supply those murderous forces with more guns and more training. The other was his letter to President Jimmy Carter asking him to stop lending support to the Salvadoran armed forces unless they gave unequivocal signs that they would indeed stop repressing their own people. Unfortunately, Romero's sacrifice put only a temporary stop to U.S. complicity with those crimes. In the Reagan years, American involvement in El Salvador grew manifold, and the "elite" units created under U.S. tutelage, especially the Atlacatl Battalion, distinguished themselves for their brutality, not by their professionalism. The Atlacatl Battalion made its debut with the El Mozote massacre, a few months after Romero's death, and completed its sorry history in November 1989, with the murder of the Jesuit fathers. That is the record we have to show for U.S. involvement in El Salvador's war.

Through the years, the message of Romero has nonetheless inspired actions for which many Americans can be proud, mostly by mounting effective campaigns to condition U.S. military aid abroad and to use the concerns of American congressional members to put pressure on foreign governments on human rights issues. This is a form of solidarity that the victims of human rights abuse do not forget, and that hold the promise for improved relations with other countries across generations. It is important, however, to draw continuing inspiration from Romero to continue those efforts and to make them even more effective, at a time when legitimate concerns for drug traffic and terrorism again threaten to wipe out considerations of human rights, democracy, and human decency in the conduct of American foreign and military policies.

The effort to put the might of the United States on the side of the poor and the oppressed is as urgent today as it has always been. If anything, it is more difficult and uphill these days, when a misunderstood patriotism and well-exploited fear of the unknown drives many honest Americans to side with militaristic and unilateral approaches to all of the world's conflicts. If we follow Romero's example, we can promote measures of defense against terrorism that are effective and just, while at the same time we insist that they must be fully consistent with long-standing American and universal values of human rights and promotion of human dignity.

Questions for Reflection

As Cardinal Rodríguez tells us, a leader is someone who has a clear idea; someone who can articulate that idea; and someone who moves forward in giving witness. How did Archbishop Romero incorporate these three ideas of leadership? In what ways was he a leader?

Archbishop Mendes speaks of the many forms of solidarity which promote awareness of institutional injustice in Latin America and of the importance of solidarity in continuing the work of Archbishop Romero. Do you know any specific examples of such solidarity groups?

The message and the witness of Monseñor Romero concerning human rights continue to be valid. Human rights are all too often violated not only in warfare or in dictatorships but also in democracies whenever corruption and lack of social consciousness predominate. Are our standards today in the Church clearly supportive of human rights?

As Dr. Zamora tells us, "Romero can inspire by the manner in which he brought together Christianity and politics." How do you understand this statement? How do you integrate your religious beliefs with politics?

Margaret Swedish quotes Archbishop Romero's second pastoral letter ("The Church, the Body of Christ in History") to illuminate his concept of Church as "a living, breathing 'space' in which the building of the reign of God was taking place. He saw not a static reality but an ever-evolving reality being molded and shaped by the same history that is the subject of God's saving action. The institution, then, as the organized structure of the Church, was also not to be static. It needs to be a body of human beings of faith constantly attentive to how God is acting in the world to bring about that reign." In practice, how did Monsignor Romero show commitment to the Church as a "living, breathing space" in which the building of the reign of God takes place?

The official documentation of the Catholic Church, especially since the Second Vatican Council, has contained clear and repeated calls to respect a preferential option for the poor. Archbishop Romero was consistent in emphasizing this option, especially in his four pastoral letters. Do you sense this same urgency in the Church today? If so, give concrete examples. If not, what specific examples might you suggest to strengthen this awareness?

About the Authors

Reverend Dean Brackley, S.J., served as priest, educator, and community organizer in inner-city parishes of the South Bronx throughout most of the 1970s and 1980s. He taught at Fordham University in 1989 and 1990, but requested reassignment to the University of Central America (UCA) in San Salvador shortly after six Jesuit priests and their housekeepers were murdered by the Salvadoran military to "punish" them for their defense of the poor and oppressed. Since 1990, Fr. Brackley has taught theology at UCA as well as chairing UCA's School for Religious Education. He also does extensive pastoral work in some of the most impoverished barrios of San Salvador. Inspired by his keen awareness of the need to communicate the immutable bonds between faith and social conscience, Fr. Brackley is working on a book that relates key themes of Ignatian spirituality to initiatives for social change. In addition to numerous speeches and journal articles on religion and society, he has written books about Christian social action, Christian social ethics, and the enormous role that Catholic social teachings play in the Church's mission in the world.

Dr. Roberto Cuéllar is Executive Director of the Interamerican Institute of Human Rights (IIHR). A native Salvadoran, he began his career defending human rights in 1975 in El Salvador by helping to form Socorro Jurídico, an organization providing legal assistance to the victims of human rights abuses. As a close collaborator and legal advisor of Archbishop Oscar Romero, he was forced to flee El Salvador after Romero was assassinated in 1980. From exile, he documented more than a thousand cases of gross human rights violations in his homeland and the surrounding region, and he submitted his evidence to both the United Nations and the Interamerican Commission on Human Rights. He began to work for the IIHR in 1985, providing human rights training to Latin American organizations and other professional services to electoral bodies, courts, religious groups, and social justice organizations throughout Central America. In the 1990s Dr. Cuéllar was an active participant in the U.N.-brokered Salvadoran and Guatemalan peace processes. He is the recipient of numerous human rights awards, including the Letelier Moffitt Human Rights Prize.

The Most Reverend Luciano Mendes de Almeida, S.J., is Archbishop of Mariana, Brazil, and former president of the Brazilian Conference of Catholic Bishops. Throughout four decades as a Jesuit priest, as Auxiliary Bishop of São Paulo, and now as Archbishop of Mariana, he has lived and ministered in the Romero tradition by relentlessly striving to improve an unjust society, especially in his work with the impoverished street children of São Paulo.

Reverend Joseph Nangle, O.F.M., is Executive Director of the Franciscan Mission Service of North America and chairperson of the U.S. Catholic Mission Association. He has also served as Associate Director for Justice and Peace at the Conference of Major Superiors of Men. Father Nangle is the coauthor of numerous reflections upon the interrelationship of faith and social justice, and is an unswerving advocate of God-given human rights and human dignity. Most recently, he has become a leader in the growing Catholic movement that seeks just and peaceful solutions to the threat of international terrorism.

The Most Reverend Oscar Andrés Cardinal Rodríguez Maradiaga, S.D.B., is Archbishop of Tegucigalpa, Honduras, and the past president of the Conference of Latin American Bishops. He served as the Vatican spokesperson to the International Monetary Fund and the World Bank on the issue of Third World debt, and he is one of the authors of *Ecclesia in America*, the 1999 papal exhortation based on the Special Synod for America. Cardinal Rodríguez has tirelessly campaigned for human rights, brokered numerous peace accords, and led rebuilding efforts following earthquakes and hurricanes—endeavors that continue the work of Archbishop Romero. In November 2002, he was awarded the Notre Dame Prize for Distinguished Service in Latin America.

Don Samuel Ruiz García, Bishop Emeritus of San Cristobal de Las Casas in the Mexican state of Chiapas, is president of the Oscar Romero International Solidarity Secretariat, of the Fray Bartolome de Las Casas Human Rights Center, and of the Center of Service and Advice for Peace in Mexico. Throughout the five decades of his ministry, Bishop Ruiz has championed the rights, welfare, and human dignity of Mexico's indigenous communities. In 1974, he organized the first National Indigenous Congress, and forged the delegates' recommendations into a comprehensive social-action program. When the Chiapas-based Zapatista National Liberation Army declared war against the Mexican Army in 1994, Bishop Ruiz single-handedly negotiated a cease-fire that prevented what would otherwise have been an appallingly bloody civil war.

Margaret Swedish is Director of the Religious Task Force on Central America and Mexico, which was founded in March 1980 two weeks before the assassination of Archbishop Romero. It was created by U.S. Catholic religious leaders in response to Romero's call for international solidarity with his persecuted people, who were suffering under the weight of military dictatorship, government repression, and horrendous social and economic inequities. For over two decades, RTFCAM has helped thousands of North Americans walk in faith-based solidarity with our sisters and brothers of Central America and Mexico. Both its mission and the interpersonal relationships it helps to foster are based on shared commitment to social justice, peaceful resolution of conflict, and faith reflections deeply rooted in the aspiration for justice, freedom from oppression, human dignity, and God-given human rights.

Dr. Rubén Zamora is a prominent Salvadoran political leader, a former professor at the Universidad Centroamerica, and one of Latin America's foremost champions of peace and social justice. While serving as Speaker of the National Assembly during and after El Salvador's twelve-year-long civil war, and as the presidential candidate of the Democratic Convergence Party in 1994 and in 1999, he steadfastly championed the God-given rights of the poor, the oppressed, and the marginalized majority of his country's citizens. He lost the presidential elections to the extreme-rightist ARENA candidates in elections "supervised" by heavily armed paramilitary forces who openly intimidated *campesino* and blue-collar voters. Nevertheless, he has seen his Democratic Convergence Party and the allied Farabundo Marti National Liberation Front win half the seats in the National Assembly less than a decade after its supporters were being machine-gunned by military death squads. Dr. Zamora remains active in Salvadoran politics, serving as a voice of moderation and reconciliation in a nation that is still dangerously polarized.

For Additional Study

Books

Bergman, Susan. *Martyrs: Contemporary Writers on Modern Lives of Faith*. Maryknoll, N.Y.: Orbis Books, 1998.

Berryman, Phillip. *Religious Roots of Rebellion: Christians in Central American Revolutions*. Maryknoll, N.Y.: Orbis Books, 1984.

———. *Stubborn Hope: Religion, Politics, and Revolution in Central America*. Maryknoll, N.Y.: Orbis Books, 1995.

Brockman, James R. *The Church Is All of You: Thoughts of Archbishop Oscar A. Romero*. Minneapolis: Winston Press, 1984.

———. *Romero: A Life*. Maryknoll, N.Y.: Orbis Books, 1989.

———. *The Violence of Love: The Pastoral Wisdom of Archbishop Oscar Romero*. Foreword by Henri J. M. Nouwen. Maryknoll, N.Y.: Orbis Books, 2004.

Dennis, Marie. *A Retreat with Oscar Romero and Dorothy Day: Walking with the Poor*. Cincinnati: St. Anthony Messenger Press, 1997.

Dennis, Marie, Renny Golden, and Scott Wright. *Oscar Romero: Reflections on His Life and Writings*. Maryknoll, N.Y.: Orbis Books, 2000.

Ellacuria, Ignacio. *Freedom Made Flesh: The Mission of Christ and His Church*. Translated by John Drury. Maryknoll, N.Y.: Orbis Books, 1976.

Galdámez, Pablo. *Faith of a People: The Life of a Basic Christian Community in El Salvador, 1970–1980*. Maryknoll, N.Y.: Orbis Books, 1986.

Golson, Richard, ed. *Fascism's Return: Scandal, Revision, and Ideology Since 1980.* Lincoln & London: University of Nebraska Press, 1998.

Lernoux, Penny. *Cry of the People: United States Involvement in the Rise of Fascism, Torture, and Murder, and the Persecution of the Catholic Church in Latin America.* Garden City, N.Y.: Doubleday, 1980.

López-Vigil, Maria. *Death and Life in Morazán: A Priest's Testimony from a War Zone in El Salvador.* Translated by Dinah Livingstone. Washington, D.C.: EPICA, 1989.

Montgomery, Tommie Sue. *Revolution in El Salvador: Origins and Evolution.* Boulder, Colo.: Westview Press, 1982.

Moreno, Juan Ramón. *Gospel and Mission: Spirituality and the Poor.* Manilla: Cardinal Bea Institute of Ateneo de Manilla University, 1995.

Nelson-Pallmeyer, Jack. *War Against the Poor: Low Intensity Conflict and Christian Faith.* Maryknoll, N.Y.: Orbis Books, 1989.

Pelton, Robert, ed. *From Power to Communion: Toward a New Way of Being Church Based on the Latin American Experience.* Notre Dame & London: University of Notre Dame Press, 1994.

Peterson, Anna L. *Martyrdom and the Politics of Religion: Progressive Catholicism in El Salvador's Civil War.* Binghampton, N.Y.: SUNY Press, 1997.

Romero, Oscar A. *Archbishop Oscar Romero: A Shepherd's Diary.* Translated by Irene B. Hodgson. Cincinnati: St. Anthony Messenger Press, 1993.

———. *Voice of the Voiceless: The Four Pastoral Letters and Other Statements.* Translated by Michael J. Walsh. Maryknoll, N.Y.: Orbis Books, 1985.

Santiago, Daniel. *The Harvest of Justice: The Church of El Salvador Ten Years After Romero.* New York: Paulist Press, 1993.

Santiago, Roberto. *Saint Romero of the Americas: A Layman's Case for Canonization of the Greatest Martyr-Prophet of the Twentieth Century.* New York: Avanti Press, 1982.

Sobrino, Jon. *Archbishop Romero: Memories and Reflections.* Maryknoll, N.Y.: Orbis Books, 1990.

———. *Jesus Christ the Liberator: A Historical-Theological Reading of Jesus of Nazareth.* Maryknoll, N.Y.: Orbis Books, 1993.

———. *The Principle of Mercy: Taking the Crucified People from the Cross.* Maryknoll, N.Y.: Orbis Books, 1994.

Sobrino, Jon, and Ignacio Ellacuria. *Companions of Jesus: The Jesuit Martyrs of El Salvador.* Maryknoll, N.Y.: Orbis Books, 1990.

Sobrino, Jon, Ignacio Martin-Baró, and Rodolfo Cardenal, eds. *La voz de los sin voz: La palabra viva de Monseñor Romero.* San Salvador: UCA Editiores, 1980.

Stanley, William. *The Protection Racket State: Elite Politics, Military Extortion, and Civil War in El Salvador.* Philadelphia: Temple University Press, 1996.

Swedish, Margaret. *Archbishop Oscar Arnulfo Romero: Prophet to the Americas.* Washington, D.C.: Religious Task Force on Central America & Mexico, 1995.

Films and Videos

Enemies of War, a film by Esther Cassidy, PBS, 1999, 57 minutes.
Killing Priests Is Good News, BBC, 1990, 57 minutes.
A Question of Conscience, Icarus/Tamouz Productions, 1990, 43 minutes.
Remembering Romero, a film by Peter Chappell, 1992, 28 minutes.
Romero, starring Raul Julia and Richard Jourdan, Trimark, 1989, 105 minutes.
Roses in December, a film by Ana Carrigan & Bernard Stone, Facets, 1982, 56 minutes.

Internet Sites

"Access to Catholic Social Justice Teachings"
   http://www.justpeace.org/
"Death & Lies in El Salvador: The Ambassador's Tale"
   http://www.creighton.edu/CollaborativeMinistry/RbtWhite.html
"Father Romero and the Treadmill of Heroism"
   http://www.creighton.edu/CollaborativeMinistry/romero-wp-3-28-80.html
"Human Rights Update"
   http://www.icomm.ca/carecen/page38.html
"The Jesuit Martyrs of El Salvador: A Research Guide"
   http://spcuna.spc.edu/library/jesuit2.html
"Martyrdom & Mercy"
   http://www.creighton.edu/CollaborativeMinistry/WPnov19.html
"Monseñor Romero-Biblioteca Virtual Miguel de Cervantes"
   http://cervantesvirtual.com/bib_autor/romero/index.html
"Oscar A. Romero Central American Refuge Center"
   http://www.icomm.ca/carecen/page25.html
"Oscar Romero: Bishop of the Poor"
   http://salt.claretianpubs.org/romero/romero.html
"A Remembrance of Archbishop Oscar Romero of El Salvador"
   http://salt.claretianpubs.org/romero/rindex.html
"Romero—BBC1 Report"
   news.bbc.co.uk/hi/english/world/americas/newsid_690000/690/36.stm
"Romero—Resources for Catholic Educators"
   http://www.silk.net/RelEd/romero.htm

"School of the Americas Watch"
  http://www.derechos.org/soaw
"Seven Sermons of Oscar Romero for Lent"
  http://www.justpeace.org/romero
"Twentieth Century Martyrs—Oscar Romero"
  http://www.stpetersnottingham.org/articles.htm
"Twenty Years After Oscar Romero Was Killed: Nobody in El Salvador Has Forgotten"
  http://www.web.net/~icchrla/Salvador/ (under Commentary)
"The UN Truth Commission on Romero's Murder"
  http://www.icomm.ca/carecen/page41.html